WAVE THREE

THE NEW ERA IN NETWORK MARKETING

Richard Poe

D0002790

P Prima Publishing
P.O. Box 1260BK
Rocklin, CA 95677

Cover photograph © IMAGE TECH/WEST COMPUTER GRAPHICS

Library of Congress Cataloging-in-Publication Data

Poe, Richard. 1958–
  Wave 3: the new era in network marketing/Richard Poe.
  p. cm.
  Includes index.
  ISBN 1-55958-501-3
  1. Multilevel marketing. I. Title II. Title: Wave three
HF5415.126.P64 1994
658.8'14—dc20

94-9089
CIP Rev

99 98 97 96 AA 19 18 17 16 15 14 13 12
Printed in the United States of America

Figure 3.1 first appeared in *Success* in June 1993. Reprinted with permission of *Success* magazine. Copyright 1993 by Hal Holdings Corporation.

The income claims made in this book by individual distributors are true, to the author's best knowledge. In no case did these distributors represent to the author that their incomes were typical for the industry or for their companies, nor does the author so claim. On the contrary, the author selected interview subjects specifically for their exceptional and unusual achievements. The earnings of average MLM distributors are obviously far lower. The author further makes no recommendation to readers regarding what companies are best to join. Companies are cited in this book for purposes of illustration only. No one should select an MLM opportunity except on the strength of his or her thorough due diligence.

To my wife, Marie

CONTENTS

FOREWORD

It is with the greatest pleasure—and pride—that I recommend this exciting and important book by Richard Poe.

I used to regard network marketing much as did other journalists. I assumed that most MLM companies were "pyramid schemes" designed to bamboozle the gullible and the naive. Imagine my consternation when one of my editors at *Success* began pressuring me to start giving serious coverage to this controversial subject in the magazine. I was skeptical, to say the least.

Of course, I had to admit that senior editor Richard Poe had a track record for being right. For some years, he wrote a back-page column for us called "The Pulse," in which he predicted future trends with often stunning accuracy. He was also an early champion among our staff of another often misrepresented industry, franchising. Poe developed the annual *Success* Gold 100 listing of the top franchise companies—now one of our most popular features. Finally, the single "Pulse" column that Poe had already written on network marketing had drawn an enthusiastic reaction from many readers. The question was, should we do more?

I was afraid Poe had gone too far this time. I feared that his seemingly boundless stores of enthusiasm had obscured his judgment.

"Some of the stories are simply too good to be true," I told him during one of Poe's many attempts to enthrall me with spectacular tales of MLM success.

But as time wore on, Poe began to convince me with a barrage of facts, figures, and credible case studies. There was just too much evidence to ignore. Some of my staffers grew alarmed at my growing interest in the subject and requested a "time out," so they could muster evidence to present to me the negative view of network marketing. I gave them all the time they needed. But all the negative articles they rounded up through our Nexus on-line service failed to persuade me. On the contrary, the almost obsessively critical slant of most press coverage on MLM proved to me that the other side of the story—the positive side—had been sorely neglected, perhaps never told at all. Why shouldn't *Success* be the first to tell it?

Success readers are different from most. They're entrepreneurs. That means they're opportunity-oriented, unafraid of risk, and always on the lookout for new ideas. They don't need or want to have their information censored by paternalistic, well-meaning magazine editors trying to protect them from risk. I decided our readers would be pleased to learn about this exciting new industry.

The extensively researched article that we eventually published in *Success* was the first positive treatment of network marketing to appear on the cover of a major national publication.

Our conclusion, in the story, was that network marketing was a powerful method of doing business that would grow in importance in the coming years. We backed up that thesis with interviews of prominent experts, such as Dr. Srikumar Rao, chairman of the marketing department of Long Island University and a 20-year student of MLM companies.

With MLM, Rao told *Success,* there are "no employees to supervise, no payrolls to meet, and you can go off on a six-month vacation and come back making money." Despite his enthusiasm, Rao evinced a strong awareness of network marketing's dark side—the overabundance of scam artists and sleazy operators. But he also observed quite sensibly that these abuses no more invalidate MLM than a few porno freaks negate all the legitimate uses of 900-number services. I heartily concur.

The story—which Poe edited—created such a sensation among our readers that we were virtually compelled to institute regular network marketing coverage in the magazine on an ongoing basis, lest we be torn asunder by avid readers hungry for more.

Poe left *Success* some time ago to become a full-time author. His presence has been sorely missed. Poe is a master storyteller. He draws you into the page and grips you with his contagious enthusiasm. Network marketing has long needed a writer like Poe with the passion to portray this most passionate of all industries.

Poe is also a born futurist. In my years of working with him, I have found his intuitions to be uncannily correct, especially regarding his prognostication of future trends. Poe's vision of a Wave-Three Revolution holds importance not only for network marketing, but for all of society. Wave-Three systems and technology form the ultimate "business incubator," allowing ordinary people to gain access to residual income and business ownership. Nowhere have I seen such a thorough and knowledgeable discussion of this phenomenon as in *Wave Three: The New Era of Network Marketing*. I believe *Wave Three* will guide many entrepreneurs to success. It will also teach many non-entrepreneurs to become self-sustaining businesspeople. Perhaps most important, it will give a powerful voice to a worthy industry which has long been denied one. *Wave Three* is surely the best-written, most insightful, and most important book ever written on the vital subject of network marketing.

Scott DeGarmo
Editor-in-Chief and Publisher, *Success*

PREFACE

"Uh . . . are you . . . Richard Poe? I mean *the* Richard Poe?"

The star-struck tremor in the caller's voice was unmistakable. I had become famous. Or rather, I had achieved *micro*-fame. When pop artist Andy Warhol predicted that everyone in the future would enjoy 15 seconds of fame, I doubt that he had network marketing in mind. But that industry is surely unequaled in the speed and lavishness with which it bestows fleeting, limited, but incredibly intense celebrity upon those it favors. I call this phenomenon *micro-celebrity*.

"I really enjoyed your article, Mr. Poe," continued my new fan in his heavy, Midwestern drawl. "It was a fine, fine article."

There was no need to ask which article he meant. By now, I was getting used to these sorts of calls. It was May 1990. My phone at *Success* magazine had been ringing off the hook for a month. A pile of pink "While You Were Out" slips overflowed across my desk. All referred to a single, one-page column I'd written called, "Network Marketing: The Most Powerful Way to Reach Consumers in the '90s."

The column's influence had grown far beyond *Success's* 400,000 regular readers. In the months ahead, I learned that thousands, perhaps millions of photocopies had been handed out across the nation by recruiters for network marketing companies—sometimes called MLM or multilevel marketing companies. Industry experts estimate that 6 to 7 million Americans work as full- or part-time network marketers. In May 1990, every one of them seemed to know who Richard Poe was.

"Welcome to network marketing," laughed John Fogg, editor of *Upline*, a leading MLM newsletter. "You're starting to get a taste of the power of word-of-mouth marketing."

Indeed I was. Months after the issue had disappeared from the newsstand, the letters kept on coming. If there were two things they all had in common, they were gratitude and anger. The writers were grateful that at last a "mainstream" business magazine had written something positive about their industry. They were angry that they'd had to wait so long for it.

> *"Why doesn't the media focus more on network marketing?"*
>
> *"I would like to see more* Success *stories on MLM."*
>
> *"Your recent article in* Success *about MLM really got my pulse racing! Where can I find more information?"*
>
> *"Thanks for a great article on network marketing. But where do I go next? Is there a book I can read on MLM?"*
>
> *"After reading your article about MLM in* Success, *I went to the library for more information. I could not find it."*
>
> *"It was with great satisfaction that this 78-year-old man read your fine article on MLM. I've been in this business since the '60s. At last, a magazine with the reputation and stature of* Success *has taken a favorable stand on our industry."*

Who were these people? How many of them were there? Why were they so passionate about network marketing? I had to find the answers.

Thus began a three-year personal odyssey, fraught with danger, adventure, intrigue, and unbelievable opportunity. Like Henry Morton Stanley penetrating Darkest Africa, I journeyed into an unknown land, a country peopled with incurable optimists, dreamers, extroverts, philosophers, and multimillionaires. I infiltrated meetings where hundreds of potential converts listened rapt to recruitment speeches, their eyes sparkling with dreams of financial freedom. I hobnobbed with celebrities, battled bureaucracies, endured the ridicule of colleagues. At the end of it all, I found the answers to all my questions. This book is the culmination of that personal quest.

It all started one morning in 1990 as I walked to work past the New York Public Library at Fifth Avenue and Forty-Second Street. A furtive-looking young man with unruly hair stood at the corner, handing out flyers.

"How would you like to quit your job, become your own boss, and build up enough residual income in a few years to support yourself for the rest of your life?" asked the flyer, or something to that effect. "If so, call this number."

I did, in fact, call the number, not because I wanted to get rich, but because, as senior editor of *Success,* I was always looking for a story. It turned out that the man on the corner was an independent distributor for something called a "network marketing" company. He was trying to recruit people into his "downline."

"Why not write a column on this strange new industry?" I mused. Little did I suspect what was in store.

As described above, the column drew an incredible response. Caught between the enthusiasm of our readers and the skepticism of some staffers, editor Scott DeGarmo encouraged a no-holds-barred debate among the staff to ascertain the truth about MLM and to decide the question of whether *Success* should continue its coverage of that industry. In the Darwinian struggle that ensued, some of my fellow editors argued that network marketing was a pyramid scam and that *Success* should steer clear of it. So heated grew the debate that I backed off the subject for over a year, wary of even mentioning the explosive words *network marketing* in any editorial meeting.

But the phones kept ringing. The readers kept clamoring. I continued my research surreptitiously, conducting interviews on the sly, sneaking to the photocopy machine to copy pertinent clips, chatting up consultants on the phone, and socking away thick sheaves of data and phone numbers deep in my file cabinet, safe from prying eyes.

At last, a year and a half after I wrote that first column, Scott DeGarmo asked me to edit a cover story on network marketing—a definitive feature that would introduce MLM to the "legitimate" business world. No other national business magazine had done anything like it (or has to this day, as far as I know).

Pulling out my secret network-marketing Rolodex, I immediately went to work assembling a crack team of writers, consultants, and experts. Valerie Free, the editor and publisher of the respected *Marketing Insights* magazine, came onboard to pen the main story. Other columns and sidebars were contributed by industry personalities such as Jerry Rubin, the '60s radical-turned-MLM prophet, and Clifton Jolley. *Upline* editor John Fogg worked tirelessly behind the scenes, providing information and contacts. Each and every article was meticulously approved for accuracy by my friend Dr. Srikumar Rao, chairman of the marketing department of Long Island University and one of the nation's leading experts on network marketing. My friend, colleague, and fellow senior editor, Duncan Maxwell Anderson, lent his brilliant editorial assistance.

The impact was immediate. It defied all expectations. Never had I seen a single article generate such intense reader interest months before it ever hit the newsstand! Word spread like electricity through the MLM rumor-mill. Faxes rolled, phones rang, voice-mail systems downloaded, electronic bulletin boards lit up like the Manhattan skyline. So many orders poured in for advance copies of the issue that we had to hire a full-time telemarketer just to take the calls! Micro-celebrity had struck again.

I left *Success* shortly thereafter. But they're still covering the network-marketing industry. Indeed, as far as I am aware, *Success* remains the only national business magazine to do so. Most Americans still don't know that network marketing even exists, nor do they understand how it's destined to change the way we live and work in the years ahead.

All this simply to illustrate that this book was written to fill a desperate, desperate need, a hunger for information that few mainstream business writers will even now dare to fill.

I suppose I should say here that I am not now nor have I ever been a network-marketing distributor. I'm still naive enough to hope that my writing career will someday provide me with all the residual income I'll ever need. But, as a journalist, network marketing intrigues me. From my first exposure to the industry, I sensed that it was more than just a business. I believe it foreshadows a future world in which men and women will no longer cower before bosses and bureaucrats, but will stand tall, like the pioneers of old, masters of their own destiny.

That's what the Wave-Three Revolution—the subject of this book—is all about. It really began over 50 years ago, when Carl Rehnborg invented network marketing—a business system designed to make it easy for anyone to become an entrepreneur. MLM's rough and ready days lasted 40 years, a formative period that I have named Wave One. Wave Two took hold in the 1980s, when PC technology made it feasible to start an MLM company from your garage. That created a groundswell of new companies. But Wave-Two network marketing still tended to work best for those who needed it least—aggressive, sales-oriented entrepreneurs.

It is only Wave Three, now making its entrance, that finally offers the masses a realistic promise of financial freedom. Through new systems and technology, Wave Three enables average men and women—not just super-salespeople—to enjoy the fruits of entrepreneurship while avoiding many of its hardships.

"If Wave Three lives up to its promise," says Michael Gerber, author of *The E-Myth,* "a whole new type of network marketing will evolve in which the distributor functions mainly as a human contact point through which the company's communications or information stream is channeled. Someone who doesn't have strong communications skills, strong selling skills, strong management skills will need them less and less. The idea is, 'You do what you do best, and we, the company, will do all the rest.'"

Wave Three will transfer massive power into the hands of common folk—the power of self-sufficiency, self-management, and self-mastery. For decades, science fiction writers have fearfully predicted man's enslavement by machine. But Wave Three networkers exploit technology to enhance and strengthen their personal liberty.

For the average reader, this book will explain what network marketing is and how to get started in it. For the hardened veteran, it introduces the Wave-Three Revolution and tells you how to use the new systems to expand your downline, swell your profits, and exploit the limitless opportunities that lurk untapped at the fringes of your existing business.

Among the many important lessons and features you'll find in *Wave Three* are:

- A checklist for measuring your personal potential for Wave-Three success
- How to identify a Wave-Three company
- How to choose a compensation plan
- The seven deadly pitfalls of beginners
- "Low-impact" prospecting and sales techniques

- A failsafe "sponsorship system" that can make any-one a leader
- How to access the greatest motivator of all
- The Wave-Three Attitude—a new psychology for winning in the Information Age

One thing this book cannot do is recommend which company you should join. I have my personal favorites, of course, but I write about them here only for the purpose of illustration. Choosing a network-marketing company is a serious business decision, for which you must exercise your own due diligence.

Above all, this book is meant to celebrate and honor the men and women of network marketing—those millions of Americans who still dare to dream big. In these troubled economic times, many have begun to question whether the American Dream can endure for another generation. You won't find such fears haunting network marketers. If our children and grandchildren find any trace of the American Dream intact when they reach adulthood, it will be, in large part, thanks to people like you, dear reader, who kept the flame alive when so many others had lost all hope.

Richard Poe

ACKNOWLEDGMENTS

Mere thanks cannot express my gratitude to my wife, Marie, for her love, support, and encouragement during the preparation of this book. Without her, it could not have been written.

The views and judgments expressed in *Wave Three: The New Era of Network Marketing* are entirely my own, as are all errors contained therein. Nevertheless, I owe my understanding of this industry to the advice and insight of many people who gave freely of their time, energy, and other resources to initiate me into the mysteries of network marketing. In particular, I thank Dr. Srikumar Rao, Clifton Jolley, Valerie Free, Jerry Rubin, Michael Senn, and Beverly Nadler. I thank also my literary agent, Ken Shelton, and his capable staff at Executive Excellence, especially Meg McMay and Trent Price; my attorney Steve Kurtz; and all the folks at Prima Publishing, including Ben Dominitz, Jennifer Basye, Andi Reese Brady, and Diane Durrett, as well as my copyeditor, Janis Paris, for all their hard work.

I especially thank Nu Skin International for its extensive support, input, and material assistance in preparing this book—assistance which in no way limited my editorial independence or my freedom to write about other companies. Special thanks go to Nu Skin's Blake Roney, Clara McDermott, Ray Beckham, Jan Hemming, Alan Jensen, Mark Walker, Robert Wakefield, Mark Yarnell, Tom and Terry Hill, Kathy Denison, and Mark Rogow.

In the roster of my many benefactors, a special place of honor is reserved for Duncan Maxwell Anderson of *Success* magazine, a true friend, whose advice, support, and brilliant editing were essential in making *Wave Three* a success. I thank Scott DeGarmo for his invaluable assistance and for his courageous advocacy of the network marketing industry.

For all their excellent newsletters and for their generous outpouring of time in helping me research this book, I thank Leonard Clements, publisher of *MarketWave* (tel. 800-688-4766 or 209-432-3834); John Milton Fogg, editor of *Upline* (tel. 804-979-4427); and Corey Augenstein, publisher of *Down-Line News* (tel. 212-355-1071).

Finally, I wish to thank all those people whose names now elude me, or whose names I never knew, who, in one way or another, have kept me hot on the trail of the Wave-Three Revolution.

INTRODUCTION

IN DAYS OF OLD, WHEN KNIGHTS WERE BOLD . . . kings, queens, and other royals had champions. These knights defended the honor of the royals, battled dragons for them, jousted on their behalf risking life and limb, waged war against their enemies, and—were there such things at the time—would probably have ridden down to the 7-Eleven on their great steeds to pick up a six-pack of Diet Pepsi for them, too.

Wave Three is written by such a champion. A modern knight in the contemporary guise of a renowned business journalist, accomplished author, and the former senior editor of *Success* magazine—off on a quest to find the Holy Grail of free enterprise.

He's found it. It's network marketing, and network marketing is what *Wave Three* is all about.

I've ghostwritten and authored a number of books on network marketing sales—more than anyone else I know of. I've also written and edited more articles on the subject than I can remember. And that's my background for saying the following:

I predict Wave Three will be the bestselling book about network marketing written to date.

I must admit—I wish I'd written *Wave Three.* I would love to have explained so clearly and so powerfully this most misunderstood concept that is revolutionizing marketing and sales the world over. Richard Poe has accomplished that task marvelously.

I have a requirement for any book I read: It must deliver to me new information, insight, and even inspiration, or I will put it down—unfinished. I read *Wave Three* cover-to-cover. And I will read it again—more than once. I will think about many ideas presented in this book for a long time. I'll be writing about them, too.

The author has the advantage of being an objective journalist, schooled in the no-nonsense colleges of New York City publishing. As I said, he is a skeptic, not easily swayed by innuendo or hearsay; he is a fact-hound who discovers truth like a heat-seeking missile while remaining open to conflicting ideas.

Poe had the courage to write about network marketing back in 1990, at the risk of his professional reputation, when all about him discouraged his every word. The result: his article, "Network Marketing: The Most Powerful Way to Reach Consumers in the '90s," became the most reprinted and most quoted piece on the profession in the 60-year history of network marketing.

Poe pioneered (ram-rodded, pushed through, struggled against all odds, fought like the devil for . . .) the first full-length positive feature on network marketing in any national magazine in America, the March 1992 issue of *Success* magazine with the headline, "34 Masters of Multi-Level Marketing Proclaim: 'We Create Millionaires'." *Success* is still reeling from the success of that one issue.

He has had more impact on network marketing sales than even he realizes. And with *Wave Three* he will multiply that impact immensely.

Network marketing is exploding as a powerful force in the new era of global marketing. Though begun in the United States, network marketing is today bigger in Japan than in America ($20 billion annually compared to $15 billion). Beyond its success as an "industry," or more properly, a profession, the impact network marketing is having and will have on all our lives is genuinely transformational—as you will discover in *Wave Three*. From the proactive and pioneering use of technology to a more human, some say even spiritual, honoring of individual effort and personal freedom, network marketing will permeate our society and culture worldwide as few concepts born of business ever have.

Wave Three reveals all of this and much more.

Whether you are not yet involved in network marketing, brand new to the business, or an established leader with a growing sales organization, *Wave Three* holds the promise and possibility of changing your life for the better—forever. Welcome to Wave Three.

John Milton Fogg
Editor of *Upline*™
Charlottesville, Virginia

WAVE THREE

THE NEW ERA IN NETWORK MARKETING

SECTION 1

ORIENTATION

Chapter 1

THE WAVE-THREE REVOLUTION

"**W**hat's wrong with me?" Terry Hill wondered. "Why do I feel so empty?"

On the surface, Hill had it all. She drove a Mercedes, vacationed in the Caribbean. At the age of 31, she was one of Xerox Corporation's top ten sales reps, raking in over $130,000 per year. Hers were the most prestigious accounts—selling high-end laserprinters to Fortune 500 companies. Every deal was worth millions. But somewhere along the line, Hill's *American dream* had collapsed into a corporate nightmare.

"I was married to my job," she says. "I slept four hours a night, got to work at 7 A.M. and left at 7 P.M. I worked every Saturday and Sunday."

Stress was eating her up from within. Every day, it seemed, Hill was fighting traffic jams, suffering through endless, stupid meetings, plowing through Kafkaesque piles of interoffice memos. In past years, she'd comforted herself by saying, "It's only temporary. Just work hard, keep your eye on the goal, and soon the rat race will be over. You'll be a success!"

But, slowly, the sickening truth had begun to dawn on her. This *was* success, the only success corporate America had to offer. "I had nowhere else to go," Hill remembers. "There were no more promotions in sales. My ratings were as high as you could get. My only choice was to go into management, which would have meant taking a pay cut, like starting over again."

THE FEVER

Although she didn't know it at the time, Hill had caught the fever—the *entrepreneurial* fever. As long as she worked for someone else, she would never be happy. The only salve for this illness was to own and manage her own business.

"I began to realize that most of my time was spent doing things that I hated," Hill recalls. "I loved to sell, but only 10 percent of my time was spent selling. The rest was dealing with the bureaucracy, trying to get orders input, fighting the administration to get something installed, trying to get bills corrected in the computer, spending days poring over commissions to make sure they were right. I wasn't in control of my own time."

For all her money, Hill was still a pawn in someone else's chess game. Each year, management reshuffled the sales force. Hill would spend an entire year wining and dining key clients, taming them like prize falcons until they ate out of her hand. Then, suddenly, Hill would be yanked away to some new territory with all new faces. Someone else would get all the repeat sales from the clients she'd developed.

"You couldn't get paid for the work you'd done a year before," she remembers. "If you wanted to make money that month, you just had to sell more product."

A *Revolution*

Hill was trapped. Unless something changed, she was doomed to run like a hamster on a treadmill till the day she retired. Hill wasn't alone in her plight. Millions shared it. In the 1980s, rising costs and plunging living standards had forced millions of baby boomers to scramble fruitlessly through 60- to 80-hour work weeks just to make ends meet. Those lucky few, like Hill, who made it to the top, often sacrificed health, family, and peace of mind. Children languished in daycare centers. Husbands and wives dragged themselves home at night, exhausted and bitter, picking wordlessly over their microwaved dinners like strangers in a skid row soup kitchen.

Hill was very fortunate to have reached her crisis at that precise moment in history. The year was 1986. A revolution was brewing across the land. Like Terry Hill, many young professionals were getting fed up. And like the American colonists in 1776, many had become angry enough to do something about it.

America Transformed

Hill and her generation weren't the first to fantasize about quitting their jobs. In pioneer days, disgruntled clerks and bankrupt shopkeepers could just load up the wagon and head out west. But for the last hundred years that option had been closed. Now, suddenly, in the 1980s, an alternative appeared, a new frontier for the restless and the bold.

Fueled by new technology and innovative marketing ideas, a small core of cutting-edge companies had set out to change the way Americans lived and worked. To corporate America, they offered a secret formula for lightning growth and global dominance. To people like Terry Hill, they offered a chance to start a business at minimal cost, to work comfortably from their homes in the bosom of their families, and—for a fortunate few—to achieve rapid wealth beyond their wildest dreams. Their ideas were revolutionary. Indeed, they have already changed Terry Hill's life beyond recognition. Before the 1990s are out, the movement they started will have utterly transformed America herself.

It's called the *Wave-Three Revolution*.

WHAT IS "WAVE THREE?"

Wave Three is the third and most powerful phase of an economic upheaval that began 60 years ago.

In 1941, a chemist named Carl Rehnborg had a brainstorm. Dr. Rehnborg was imprisoned in a Chinese internment camp during the 1920s, where his starvation diet impressed upon him the value of nutrition. Later, Rehnborg invented a new food supplement derived from alfalfa, watercress, parsley, and various vitamins and minerals. He started a company to sell it, called Nutrilite Products, Inc.

Nutrilite still exists today, as a subsidiary of Amway Corporation. And it still makes an excellent product. But, if history remembers Rehnborg, it will not be for his nutritional innovations. Rehnborg's most lasting achievement will surely be the impact he had on the quality of life itself.

Wage Slavery

Until Rehnborg came along, most people were trapped in a system of wage slavery. They traded their labor for *linear income*—a fixed wage or hourly rate tied directly to the amount of time they spent on the job.

Of course, you can make good money through linear income. Some consultants charge hundreds or even thousands of dollars per hour. But they must work that hour in order to get it! And if they get sick, they'd better not stay sick too long. Nobody pays a consultant for lying in bed.

"You can never be free as a professional selling your hours for dollars," says Jerry Rubin, a frontline distributor for Life Extension International based in Arlington, TX. "You may get $100 an hour, but you've got to show up and be there every hour."

When you work for linear income, you must jump to another's commands. If your boss wants you at your desk by nine in the morning, you'd better be there. If your client wants you to catch the Red-Eye to LA to make an early meeting, don't miss that plane! As in the days of slavery, your master decides where your physical body will be at every hour of the working day.

That's why the wealthiest business moguls in history have always sought to escape the slavery of linear income. They accomplish this by leveraging the time and energy of others—leaving themselves free to plot grand strategies, start new businesses, or just enjoy life!

As John Paul Getty put it, "I would rather have one percent of the efforts of a hundred people than a hundred percent of my own efforts."

Residual Income

But how do you gain the benefits of a hundred people's efforts?

Getty was talking about *residual income*. That is income that keeps coming in, year after year, long after you've finished the work. Hit songwriters, bestselling authors, and wealthy investors have always enjoyed the luxury of residual income. But common folk have been left out in the cold.

That is, until Carl Rehnborg came along.

Rehnborg's system allowed ordinary people to build up a sales network that could theoretically keep on producing income for them long after they had retired from the business. It opened the door to financial freedom for millions of Americans.

And it ushered in Wave One of the *network-marketing revolution*.

WHAT IS NETWORK MARKETING?

"Network marketing" is not defined in any standard dictionary of business terms. Nor do network marketers themselves agree on what it means. For lack of any clear standard, I suggest the following definition: "Any method of marketing that allows independent sales representatives to recruit other sales representatives and to draw commissions from the sales of those recruits."

That's how Rehnborg's company worked. Nutrilite Products, Inc. employed no sales force. Instead, Rehnborg recruited an army of independent distributors. With this system, he could roll out a national sales force without paying a penny in salaries or overhead. He didn't even have to cough up commission payments until after his distributors made a sale!

Just as important, the new system relieved Rehnborg of the sheer headache of recruiting and hiring thousands of salespeople. The distributors did it all themselves! The more recruits they brought in, the more money they made. Rehnborg had ignited an unstoppable chain reaction. His growing sales network quickly made him a rich man.

Rehnborg's company allowed distributors to draw commissions only from those they personally recruited. It was a "one-level" company. But today's network-marketing firms often allow distributors to draw commissions from several levels or "generations" of recruits. In other words, they give you a percentage of sales from recruits who were recruited by *your* recruits, and so on.

For that reason, network marketing is often called "multilevel marketing" or MLM for short.[1]

Geometric Growth

"What would you rather have—$100,000 or a penny that doubles every day for a month?"

---

1. Some industry purists would like to abolish the terms MLM and "multilevel marketing." They believe that "network marketing" sounds more sophisticated. All three expressions really mean the same thing. For the sake of variety, I will, in this book, continue to use them all interchangeably, as do most people in the industry.

Network marketers have been using this sales pitch for decades. The right answer is that you want the penny. Because, after 31 days, that penny will have multiplied to over *21 million dollars* through the magic of geometric growth.

In network marketing, your *downline*—all the people whom you recruit, whom your recruits recruit, and so on—theoretically grows in a similar geometric progression. For instance, let's say you recruit five people in your first month, and each of them recruits five more in the second month, and so on. In six months, you'll theoretically have 19,530 people in your *organization*—another term for "downline."

A typical network marketing company will give you a commission on all product sold at wholesale to those 19,530 distributors. So, if each one buys only $100 of inventory each month, and if you receive a 10 percent commission from each, that means you will earn $195,300 a month!

Herein lies the source of MLM's incredible mystique. For reasons I will explain later, few ever achieve this level of income. But it remains the network marketer's perennial dream to retire a millionaire in a few short years, collecting massive monthly commissions ever after.

Rags to Riches

For Ralph Oats, geometric growth proved a reality. Network marketing opened the door to his elusive American dream. For 23 years, Oats drove a truck for $35,000 a year. It meant long hours—sometimes days—on the road and far from home. The work was tedious, thankless, pointless. Oats burned with resentment. But trucking was all he knew. He was trapped.

"Every time I wanted to buy something," recalls his wife Cathy Oats, "Ralph would tell me how many miles he had to drive to make that amount of money."

Then Cathy discovered network marketing. She started selling water filters part-time. At first, Ralph grumbled, thinking she was wasting her time. But when Cathy brought in $14,000 after only four months of part-time work, his objections died in his throat.

Ralph quit his trucking job, and the two became partners. They cleared $100,000 in the first year. Six years later, the couple was worth a cool $7 million. Although they retired and moved to Florida, their wealth just kept on growing. They earned $1 million in residual income during the first two years of their retirement.

It's Not Easy

Of course, most network marketers don't make that much money. Attrition usually knocks out 90 percent of your distributors before they make any money for you. The geometric progression tends to peter out by the third or fourth level. And, in most plans, a distributor has to invest a lot of money up front in order to stay competitive.

In short, network marketing is a real business, with all the problems and risks of real business. It's not a lottery. The way to succeed is to put in a lot of work, a certain amount of money, and a great deal of perseverance. It won't happen overnight. But if you stick with it, you'll find what you seek.

Ponzi Scheme? Pyramid Scam?

Of course, Terry Hill, our unhappy Xerox saleswoman, had heard all about network marketing. Or rather, she had read about it in newspapers and magazines. Most of the stories were lurid exposés. Journalists seldom wrote about MLM without resorting to words like "pyramid scam," "Ponzi scheme," and "chain letter." To the media, network marketing companies were criminal conspiracies preying on the greed of gullible minorities, dopey housewives, and disgruntled garage mechanics. They portrayed MLM recruiters as fast-talking hucksters in plaid suits and patent leather shoes. Like most respectable sales professionals, Hill took these press reports at face value. She shunned network marketing as if it were leprosy.

But Hill wanted her own business. And as she explored the available options, she found them limited. She'd already tried insurance sales. There was good money in that business, but Hill always felt she was pushing something on people that they didn't really want. Then there was franchising. She could choose the business she wanted and set herself up as her own boss. But first she'd have to fork over the price tag for a franchise, which might range anywhere from $50,000 to $300,000 or more. That meant going into heavy debt.

Then Hill saw an ad in a newspaper for a network-marketing opportunity. Instantly, warning lights flashed in Hill's mind: "Ponzi scheme," "pyramid scam," "don't be a sucker!" She almost found herself turning the page. But then she stopped. What did she have to lose by talking to these people? After all, she was a smart, Fortune 500 professional. She could take care of herself. If it was a scam, she'd see through it in a minute.

"I decided to go into it with an open mind," says Hill.

Her openness was destined to make her a millionaire in only five years.[2]

Total Financial Freedom

Today, Hill presides over a global empire with over 5,000 distributors throughout North America and the Far East.

---

2. Terry Hill's income claims are true, to the author's best knowledge, as are all income claims made in this book by individual distributors. However, in no case did these distributors represent to the author that their incomes were typical for the industry, or for their companies, nor does the author so claim. On the contrary, the author selected interview subjects specifically for their outstanding achievements.

She can work as hard as she likes on any given day, or as little as she likes. If she decides to disappear for a month to Tahiti, her downline is still chugging away like crazy when she gets back.

"It's like coming out of prison," says Hill. "The personal freedom is astounding. For the first time in my life, I know I can live wherever I want to live, do whatever I want to do."

Hill's new freedom allowed her to do something else her old schedule would never have permitted—fall in love and get married. And unlike most double-income couples, Hill and her husband spend every day together. After seeing the success of her Nu Skin business, Hill's new husband quit his job as a successful stockbroker for Merrill Lynch. Today, the two work as partners.

Time Freedom

Even for that vast majority of network marketers who make far less money than Terry Hill, MLM provides a level of *time freedom* they would never find elsewhere.

Take Marjorie Musselman. The biggest monthly commission check she ever got was for $2,800. Most of her checks are for just a few hundred dollars. But Musselman's network-marketing income helped support her family when her husband was laid off. The extra money she earns keeps her family's bills paid and allows them to afford trips and other small luxuries. And, unlike other part-time employment she might have taken, Musselman's network-marketing business allows her to be the boss. She can work at home and make her own hours. And her residual income keeps flowing in, even if she takes a couple of weeks off.

Most network marketers are like Musselman. They're not out to get rich, and they probably never will. But for them, as well as for people like Terry Hill, MLM represents their last, best hope for financial freedom.

THE EVOLUTION OF WAVE THREE

"Network marketing is a far more mature industry today than it was when I was actively involved," says Dr. Edgar Mitchell, Apollo 14 lunar module pilot and the sixth man to walk on the moon.

Although no longer an active distributor, Mitchell remains a passionate advocate of network marketing. The former astronaut has worked two different MLM businesses since 1987 and still consults network marketing companies on motivational issues. To this day, Mitchell continues drawing residual income from one of his downlines.

"I've been a pioneer and explorer all my life," says Mitchell, "in my military career, as an astronaut, and in the network-marketing industry. I get into things during the tough, pioneering stage, when you're still trying to find out what the rules are and make them work."

Network marketing is only now emerging from what Mitchell calls its "tough, pioneering" days. Since the industry began over 60 years ago, it has evolved through three distinct phases. The first ended in 1979, when the Federal Trade Commission ruled that Amway was a legitimate business—not a pyramid scam. That ended "Wave One"— the long gray-market or "underground" phase of network marketing.

Then came Wave Two. New technology sparked an explosion of network marketing startups in the 1980s. Thousands of new companies sprang into business overnight. Millions of Americans entered the MLM sales force.

But the technology was immature. Like those VCRs that require an Einstein to program them, Wave-Two network marketing proved too difficult and complicated for most people. As with the early VCRs, the technology just wasn't ready for the market.

"I developed a voice mail system specifically tailored for network-marketing companies," Mitchell remembers.

"But in those early days, only the leaders recognized the value of my system. The public coming on board for the first time was really not familiar with voice mail and did not know how to use it effectively."

Eschewing technology, Wave-Two network marketers relied mainly on their own personal talents. To excel, you had to be extraordinary. Distributors were expected to single-handedly stockpile inventory, fulfill product orders, keep track of all the paperwork, prospect for new recruits, and stay up all night taking phone calls from angry or depressed people in their downlines. Wave-Two distributors were encouraged to hold mass meetings in hotels and to speak before crowds—despite the fact that social psychologists have discovered that most people fear public speaking more than death.

In short, Wave-Two distributors had to be consummate entrepreneurs. And most people just *are not*.

Wave Three Is User-Friendly

Wave Three has changed all that. Like the VCR manufacturers, network-marketing companies have been working behind the scenes to simplify their systems. Now their labors bear fruit.

Today, the most advanced VCRs are easy to program. You just talk to them. You say out loud the time and date of the program you want to record, and the machine records it.

The lesson? As technology advances, it becomes more user-friendly.

So it is with the Wave-Three organization. The most advanced network-marketing companies today stress simplicity above all. They use computers, management systems, and cutting-edge telecommunications to make life as easy as possible for the average distributor. They have taken Rehnborg's dream to its logical conclusion.

For decades, network marketers have been promising financial freedom to the masses. But only with the advent of Wave Three has that promise been fully realized.

LET THE SYSTEM DO THE WORK

Wave-Three technology takes away the need for extraordinary people. In today's Wave-Three organization, distributors rely upon a twenty-first-century network of systems, procedures, media, and technology that simplifies, standardizes, and automates the most difficult aspects of the business.

A new distributor no longer has to "wing it" when he or she pitches the first prospect. The prospect is put on a three-way phone call with an experienced recruiter and the distributor listens quietly to learn how it's done. Or the distributor can simply lend the prospect a professionally produced 30-minute recruiting video.

No longer do distributors need to stockpile their own inventory and keep track of all the paperwork. They simply direct customers to a toll-free 800 number. The company fulfills the order, credits the distributor for the sale, and spits out a computerized commission check at the end of the month.

Gone are the days when each rank-and-file networker was expected to act as leader, mentor, public speaker, and champion motivator for his whole downline. The Wave-Three networker invites recruits over for a televised pep talk from the top trainer in the company broadcast direct to the living room via satellite.

Complex on the Inside, Simple on the Outside

Each new support system that comes on line makes network marketing a little easier. And each innovation opens network marketing to a larger group of people.

The list of new technologies just keeps growing. Three-way calling, teleconferences, and "dropshipping"—the use of computerized, automated fulfillment systems—have become standard tools for today's network marketer. Fax broadcasting and voice-mail systems now let distributors deliver instructions direct to every person in their downlines. PCs print out envelope labels for mailing lists with thousands of names. Do you want to go global? Wave-Three companies take care of all the customs, taxes, currency conversion, and other hassles of international business. You just go in and make money.

All this technology takes time, effort, and money to install and operate. But the company—not the individual distributor—takes care of all that. A Wave-Three company is like one of the new, voice-activated VCRs. On the *inside,* those VCRs are filled with complex microcircuitry. But, on the *outside,* they display only a few simple buttons. Likewise, the "inside" of a Wave-Three organization is packed with computing power and complex management systems. But for the distributor, the procedure gets simpler and simpler all the time.

The Human Factor

Paradoxically, all this computerization enhances and magnifies the importance of the human element—the value of each individual distributor.

As computers take over more and more of the work that people used to do, they free up human beings to focus on those things people do best—dream, plan, strategize, solve problems, and interact with other people. Wave-Three distributors will discover ways of being productive that have never existed.

In every industry, the human factor is being similarly unleashed by systems and automation. But in most industries the unleashing is accomplished through layoffs. No high-tech workplace has integrated the human factor more quickly and successfully than the Wave-Three organization.

WHY DOES THE MEDIA IGNORE THE WAVE-THREE REVOLUTION?

Don't worry. It won't be able to much longer.

Intentionally or not, the media has tended to ignore positive news about network marketing. Successful companies like Amway and Mary Kay Cosmetics are often written about in mainstream business articles, but seldom referred to as network-marketing or MLM companies. Those forbidden phrases mainly crop up in *negative* stories, about companies that are being sued or investigated.

But, as Wave Three evolves, it's getting harder for the media to ignore the obvious. *Success* magazine broke the ice in March, 1992, with its ground-breaking cover story on MLM. Since then, *Success* has delighted readers by providing the first regular coverage of the industry in any mainstream business magazine.

I believe *Success* has opened the floodgates to what will soon be an inundation of positive media coverage.

The Best-Kept Secret in Corporate America

Network marketers have long blamed journalists for the media blackout on their industry. But reporters aren't always to blame. Even the most well-meaning journalists must rely on their contacts in the business world for information. And the growing success of network marketing has surely been one of the best-kept secrets in corporate America. As a business reporter, I can personally attest to the extraordinary difficulty in getting large corporations to admit that they are using network marketing—even when they are.

"We are not a network-marketing company!" declared one PR spokesman for a major company when I called him in connection with this book.

Since I knew from other sources that his sales force did in fact use an MLM compensation plan, I asked him what he meant.

"I mean that we're not one of these companies that works like a pyramid scheme," he explained, "where you make money by recruiting people instead of by selling products."

What an answer! The man had redefined the term "network marketing" to mean *frontloading*—an illegal practice in which distributors compel new recruits to stock exorbitant amounts of inventory, far more than they're capable of selling. Companies that stoop to such tactics can indeed make money whether or not any product is ever sold at retail. But they are also subject to prosecution! If that was the real definition of network marketing, the entire industry would be up on charges. No wonder he wouldn't admit to it!

Word games like this are endemic in the corporate world. They obscure the truth and keep reporters guessing. I have heard company spokesmen vehemently deny that they were using network marketing simply on the grounds that their company pays commissions on one level only. They seem unaware that Carl Rehnborg's Nutrilite— widely recognized as the first MLM company in history— also paid out on only one level!

Deny it though they might, these companies have embraced network marketing because it works. By the time this remarkable technique comes fully out of the closet, we may all be shocked at how pervasive its underground influence has grown behind the scenes.

THE LESSON OF FRANCHISING

Don't be dismayed by the controversy surrounding network marketing. New ideas are always attacked and rejected at first. In its early days, franchising endured similar abuse from the press and from the corporate world, and for almost identical reasons.

It all started back in the 1950s, when McDonald's, Midas Muffler, and a handful of other daring companies discovered that they could grow ten times faster than conventional firms. Instead of shelling out millions of dollars to build and operate new stores, they let independent "franchisees" do it for them. And the franchisees had to pay for the privilege!

It seemed like a great idea. But the media attacked like hungry barracuda. Exposés featured destitute families who'd lost their life savings through franchising schemes. Attorneys general in state after state condemned the new marketing method. Some Congressmen actually tried to outlaw franchising entirely.

How quickly things change! Today, franchises account for 35 percent of all retail sales in the United States. Many are among the top-rated public companies on the New York Stock Exchange. At a time when most segments of the U. S. economy remained stagnant, sales through franchised outlets reached $803.2 billion in 1992 . . . a 6 percent increase over the previous year.

Inherent Strengths

Franchising survived the media onslaught for one reason—it works. And it works better than the alternatives. Network marketing will prevail for the same reason. Its inherent strengths give it a devastating advantage over conventional companies.

Sort the Chaff from the Grain

Of course, network marketing, like franchising or any other business, has had more than its share of sleazy operators. But there are some very simple ways to sort the scams from the legitimate firms. If you wish to become a network marketer, you must do your homework. The wise entrepreneur will conduct a thorough research before climbing into bed with any company. Chapter 3 contains a reliable methodology for sorting the chaff from the grain.

DON'T GIVE UP

"Like many Americans, I was deeply suspicious of MLM," writes former '60s radical Jerry Rubin in *Success*.[3]

Back in the 1960s, America knew Rubin as a wild-eyed revolutionary, notorious for dropping hundreds of one-dollar bills on the floor of the New York Stock Exchange and for going on trial with the Chicago Seven. In the 1980s, the press dubbed him the "Yippie turned Yuppie" after Rubin donned a three-piece suit and started raking in money hosting yuppie networking parties in chic New York nightclubs.

But like so many smug high-rollers in the 1980s, Rubin was headed for a rude awakening. It came with the stock market crash of 1987. Rubin lost $700,000 overnight. At the same time, his nightclub business started falling off. "Married baby boomers didn't have time for that anymore," he recalls. "What could I do? How was I going to support my 2-year-old daughter and 1-year-old son?"

A Humbling Experience

Rubin was ruined. Each day, he sat alone in his office, sifting through business opportunity ads in the paper. One day, something caught Rubin's eye—an ad for a new network marketing company called Omnitrition, which sold vitamin drinks. At first, Rubin dismissed it.

---

3. Rubin's quotes on pages 20–21 are reprinted from *Success* magazine.

"In 1983, I'd gotten burned by an MLM company that filed Chapter 11 bankruptcy six months after I joined," he explains. "From then on, I avoided MLM like the plague."

Rubin had laughed while his friends Richard and Carol Kall joined one network-marketing company after another. Bad luck seemed to follow them like a cloud. Each company they joined promptly went out of business. Rubin thought they were suckers. But he had to admire their persistence.

"The Kalls never gave up," he says. "Years later, Richard finally struck pay dirt with a company called Nu Skin. Today he's a multimillionaire. The Kalls' persistence had paid off, whereas my cynicism had gotten me nowhere. It gave me a lot to think about."

Rubin decided to give MLM one last chance. He answered the ad for Omnitrition. "In my first year," he writes, "I became one of the highest-grossing distributors in the industry."

Today, Rubin has returned to preaching revolution. *Capitalist* revolution!

"Just as in the '60s," he says, "the baby boomers still desire freedom above all. In the '90s, I predict they'll finally achieve it through network marketing."

The Flee Generation

"If the '70s were the Me Decade," opines Rubin, "and the '80s were the Greed Decade, the '90s will be called the *Flee Decade*. Baby boomers will flee the corporate world in droves, crying, 'I can't take it anymore! I want to be in charge of my life! My time!' "

Rubin might just be on to something. But, of course, for millions of his generation, unemployment will not be a matter of choice. It will be a hard and unavoidable reality. Network marketing may prove to be one of the few avenues to personal success left open once the turbulent economics of the 1990s have run their course.

QUIT BEFORE YOU'RE FIRED!

"The white collar displacement of the 1990s will make the blue collar displacement of the 1980s pale by comparison," says leading economist Paul Zane Pilzer.

In the last ten years, millions lost their jobs through mergers, acquisitions, downsizings, and plant closings. Don't look for much relief in the years ahead. The current recession is no ordinary crimp in the business cycle. Fundamental changes are sweeping every sector of the economy. And one of the by-products of this change will be massive, long-term unemployment.

One reason is that technology has made many jobs obsolete, from the factory worker displaced by automated production lines, to the middle manager nudged out by computerized office networks.

"Companies are producing the same basket of goods and services with fewer and fewer employees," says Pilzer. "Massive layoffs with increased productivity! In the next few years, we're going to see fantastic economic growth. But we'll also see 20 percent unemployment. Sounds like a contradiction. But that's the reality!"

Permanent Underemployment

Imagine the despair of fulltime farmhands when mechanical reapers and gasoline-powered tractors appeared in the cornfields. Imagine the plight of horse-dealers and buggy-makers when Henry Ford brought out his mass-produced automobiles. Then you will grasp the fate in store for those workers and executives who fail to adapt to tomorrow's new *nonmaterial economy* (as the Club of Rome recently dubbed it).

Experts foresee permanent *underemployment* for many white-collar workers.

"For a fast-growing number of managers and professionals," says *Fortune* magazine, "work is now a concatenation of stints, ranging from two weeks to two years. . . . At least 125,000 professionals labor as temps every day. Their share of the $25 billion annual temporary work market has doubled [in 1993]."

The Contingent Workforce

More and more white-collar workers are being forced into what *Fortune* calls the *contingent workforce*. Consisting of temps, part-time workers, consultants, and the self-employed, the contingent workforce is growing at a staggering rate. According to Richard Belous, chief economist of the National Planning Association, this work force is now 45 million strong, having grown 57 percent since 1980. [This is] "three times faster than the labor force as a whole," according to *Fortune*.

White-Collar MLM

Many of those underemployed professionals are going straight into network-marketing companies. The same technology that eliminated their jobs in the Fortune 500 is now creating opportunities in the expanding Wave-Three sector.

Recruiters are hard at work reaping Corporate America's human castoffs. Wave-Three networkers target doctors, lawyers, CPAs, stockbrokers, and corporate presidents, tired of the rat race.

THE AMWAY DECADE

At least two of the world's foremost financial forecasters have predicted that network-marketing companies will thrive in the troubled times ahead.

James Dale Davidson is an advisor to nations and presidents, an economic confidante of both George Bush and Bill Clinton. His colleague and co-author, Lord William Rees-Mogg, a member of the British House of Lords and onetime editor of the *Times* of London, counsels some of the world's wealthiest investors.

In past books, this twosome stunned the world with their eerily accurate predictions. Among other forecasts, they foretold the 1987 stock market crash, the fall of Communism, the U.S. real-estate bust, the S & L crisis, and the bursting of the Japanese bubble. In their latest book, *The Great Reckoning: Protect Yourself in the Coming Depression,* they predict that the 1990s will be remembered as "the Amway Decade."

"A type of business that prospers in hard times is the informal business run from home. . . ." they write. "The 1990s will be a decade of Tupperware parties, Avon ladies, and Amway dealers." All three companies use network marketing.

THE MLM JUGGERNAUT

Corporate America has already taken some serious drubbings at the hands of network marketers.

In 1987, AT&T seemed invincible. But only five years later, the mighty monolith had surrendered a whopping 15 percent of its long-distance market share to MCI and US Sprint. What did these two upstarts have in common? Both used MLM to market their services.

In market after market, network marketers are taking the Fortune 500 head-on. Many of America's largest corporations have already quietly decided that it's better to switch than fight. Colgate Palmolive, Gillette, and Coca-Cola are among those who have launched pilot MLM programs in some product categories. Two of the nation's leading direct sales organizations, Avon and Fuller Brush, have both switched to MLM programs after losing many of their top performers to network marketing competitors.

"There's no better way today to get your product right in the consumer's face," concedes William Plikaitis, group manager for US Sprint's Consumer Services Group.

GLOBAL DOMINANCE

Few companies better illustrate the relentless might of network marketing than Amway Corporation, based in Ada, Michigan. Most press coverage about Amway fails to mention the words "network marketing." But there is no denying the company's incredible success.

Founded in 1959, Amway is one of the oldest companies in network marketing. Yet, its aggressive program of Wave-Three innovation has caused Amway's sales to more than double since 1990—exceeding $4.5 billion in the fiscal year ending August 31, 1993.

The international behemoth has more than 500 manufacturing subsidiaries, over two million independent distributors, and offers over 12,000 products and services, ranging from shampoo and kitchen cleansers to household appliances and long-distance phone service. Amway founders Jay Van Andel and Rich DeVos hold eleventh place on the 1993 Forbes 400 list of America's richest people.

While other U.S. corporations whine about Japan's impregnable trade barriers, Amway's Japanese subsidiary boasts annual sales approaching the $1 billion mark. The secret is Amway's MLM compensation structure, which holds a forbidden fascination for the workaday Japanese "salaryman."

"The opportunity to escape Japan's rigid seniority system . . . lures younger distributors in their 20s and early 30s to join Amway," said a September 21, 1990, article in the *Wall Street Journal* (which typically left out the terms MLM or "network marketing"). "In a society where building one's *jinmyaku,* or network of human contacts, is everything, selling a product through acquaintances works particularly well."

It's Coming

There's no doubt about it. Wave Three is coming.

Its advent has already been felt. Its final victory will be unmistakable. Unlike previous waves of network marketing, Wave Three will take Corporate America by frontal assault. In future years, when a thousand TV channels compete for our attention, when every consumer is numbed to the core by the ceaseless bombardment of high-impact advertising, only network marketing will pierce the cocoon of consumer apathy. Its influence will pervade every household. Its mark will be felt in every corporate boardroom.

Those companies that have worked early to establish their Wave-Three infrastructures will dominate the landscape in decades to come. And those observant networkers who have watched and waited for the change will know exactly where to find the best opportunities.

This book will help you in that search.

American Dream

For those who value the American spirit of enterprise, Wave Three offers a shining beacon of hope. In an age when bureaucrats intone darkly about the need for government-managed industrial policy, when small business is taxed beyond endurance, when giant corporations meld into hemisphere-spanning supermonopolies, some have speculated that the age of individual enterprise is dead. The American dream is obsolete, they say. Our children must accept a future of ever-shrinking living standards, increasing regimentation, and limits to growth.

Yet, like an elemental force of nature, network marketing has risen from the soil and roots of America's heartland, boldly promising wealth, freedom, and limitless horizons to those with the courage to seek them out. In network marketing, the American spirit of free enterprise finds its purest incarnation today. Many will be tested in that heady arena in the years ahead. Perhaps you would like to be one of them. If so, this book was written for you.

Chapter 2

Know Thyself

S ince its premier in April 1994, everyone has been talking about CBS's new hit show "704 Hauser." A kind of reverse "All in the Family," the sitcom features a liberal black father locking horns every week with his 20-year-old Republican son. As popular as it is, few of the show's fans realize that producer Norman Lear modeled the Republican son on a real-life "black conservative" named Armstrong Williams.

"I talk to Norman every day," says Williams. "They Fed-Ex scripts to me and I send my comments by fax. We've had brainstorming sessions where I just sit and talk for three hours and they tape me."

Williams is no stranger to celebrity. His radio talk show, "The Right Side," which airs on WOL-AM in Washington D.C., has long been one of the hottest in the country. His commentaries appear on the op-ed pages of *USA Today, Newsday,* and the *Wall Street Journal.* A self-made millionaire, Williams recently bought out the successful Georgetown public relations firm, The Graham Williams Group, from his partner, Stedman Graham, a man well-known to tabloid readers as Oprah Winfrey's fiancé. But Williams wasn't always so prosperous or well-connected.

"MLM gave me my start," he says. "The money I made in network marketing is still working for me today. Many of the people who were in my downline are the same network I use today for business and political connections all over the country."

Williams made his first big money as a distributor for Dick Gregory's Bahamian Diet, a network-marketing company that flourished in the mid-80s. But MLM gave Williams far more than money. It steeled his character. It prepared him mentally and spiritually for his biggest trial—and his greatest success.

When Williams first took to the radio air waves, he was one of the few African-American media figures who dared to openly preach patriotism, morality, and hard work. Every day that he went on the air, callers attacked him as a sell-out, an "Uncle Tom," a "Whitey lover," a traitor to his race.

"I was beginning to question my own beliefs," says Williams. "It was traumatic. I couldn't sleep at night. It was affecting my work. I met with my staff and told them I couldn't do it anymore."

But Williams hung in there. What kept him going was his training in network marketing.

"In MLM, you gotta be an original thinker," says Williams. "You gotta know who you are and stick to your beliefs, no matter what people say."

Every day that Williams walked into the sound studio, he reminded himself of the late nights he'd spent on the phone, coaxing people to join his downline.

"In network marketing, I learned that you had to be patient with people," he says. "I learned that you gotta hang in there with them."

Williams realized that those abusive callers who plagued him everyday on his radio show were little different from many of the people whom he used to recruit for Dick Gregory's Bahamian Diet. They were angry at life, frustrated by their own failure, and looking desperately for a way out. In network marketing, Williams had learned that it was often those prospects who cried "Pyramid scam!" and "Rip-off!" the loudest who proved in the end to be the most zealous recruits. Why should it be different with his radio listeners?

"When I went into the sound studio, I looked at where I was in my life," says Williams, "and I looked at where my critics were in their lives, and then I knew I must be doing something right. When they phoned in, I would ask them what they did for a living, and they were either on welfare or didn't have a job."

Williams knew in his heart that he had something worthwhile to teach his listeners, even if they didn't always want to hear it. So he ignored their insults and kept right on preaching. Now millions listen attentively to Williams' views, every week on "704 Hauser"! He still gets plenty of angry phone calls. But he gets a lot more respectful ones these days.

Do You Have What It Takes?

Network marketing requires no special skills or gifts. You need no college degrees, nor inside connections. You don't even need that much money. But one thing you need is strength of character. To make it big in MLM is one of the hardest tasks you can undertake. Often, you must go without sleep, work without pay, and yield up your last ounce of strength before catching a glimpse of the prize. Often, you must push on despite the insults and discouragement of friends, relatives, and even spouses. Most surrender long before they reach the goal.

But a chosen few succeed. Like Armstrong Williams, those who stay the course walk away with far more than money. As long as they live, they can call on hidden stores of experience, strength, and self-assurance. They can do what others cannot. They are a Delta Force of human achievement, an elite.

THE WAVE-THREE ATTITUDE

So what about Wave Three? Didn't we spend the last chapter explaining how automation and new management systems have simplified network marketing and made the business easier to work? We did and they have.

However, no amount of automation will ever eliminate the need for human effort. Ultimately, it is people who make network marketing work. In the Wave-Three organization, support systems of all kinds will take up the slack for human failings. But, paradoxically, they will also strip away the last excuses for procrastination and low productivity.

Wave-Three distributors have more time and opportunity than any previous generation of network marketers for confronting the hard challenges of face-to-face selling. With that privilege comes the responsibility to meet each trial with courage, optimism, and decisive action. For, in these changing times, when technology's march brings into question man's very role in the drama of industry, it falls to the Wave-Three distributor, more than to any other worker today, to demonstrate what the "human element" can really do.

It was the Wave-Three attitude that drove our forebears to cross dangerous oceans, when it would have been safer to hug the shore and ply familiar trade routes. The Wave-Three attitude sent men to the moon, when automated space probes could have collected just as many samples. Technology will never become a crutch so long as people use it only as a gateway to greater and greater levels of exertion and achievement.

"The whole purpose of technology," says former astronaut Edgar Mitchell, "is to free up human creativity. Technology does the scut work, the paperwork. It handles the information, so humans are left free to do what they do best."

The Right Stuff

When they went to consult the Delphic oracle, the ancient Greeks were confronted by a mysterious admonition engraved over the doorway to the temple. It read: "Know thyself."

This advice holds true for those modern-day "initiates" who seek admission to the "rites" of network marketing. With the advent of Wave Three, you no longer need to be a supersalesperson or an inspired public speaker to make it in MLM. But you do need to cultivate the Wave-Three attitude. Probe your heart. In the following pages, I provide a road-map for that quest, a checklist of personal traits you will need to succeed in Wave-Three network marketing.

If you don't have these traits already, don't despair. Every one of them can be acquired through conscious effort.

Trait #1: A Positive Outlook

To succeed in MLM, you must become a positive thinker. Without a relentlessly positive outlook, you can neither sell nor recruit. Your business will shrivel and die at the first onslaught of adversity. Like the legendary UCLA basketball coach John Wooden, veteran networkers understand that success comes not from avoiding problems, but from dealing with each problem courageously. "Things turn out best," says Wooden, "for the people who make the best of the way things turn out."

Richard Brooke was a typical negative thinker. Although his parents were affluent, college-educated ranchers in California, Brooke's downbeat attitude doomed him to early failure in life.

"My parents divorced when I was 17," says Brooke. "I hated school. I didn't study and skipped a lot of classes. I barely graduated, with a D average, and so I didn't even try for college."

For a while, Brooke thought it might be nice to be a forest ranger. But then a ranger told Brooke he'd first need to get a college degree. Even then, warned the ranger, only 300 applicants were selected per year out of 3,000.

"A nanosecond after he told me that," recalls Brooke, "I decided that I couldn't be one of those 300."

Brooke was right. He couldn't, because he believed he couldn't.

"Whether you think you can or think you can't," said Henry Ford, "you are right."

After spending four years cutting chickens on an assembly line for $3.05 an hour, Brooke decided to try network marketing. He joined a company that was selling gasoline additives that improved car mileage. Brooke worked hard at his MLM business. But three years later, it was still bringing in less than $4,000 per year.

What was the problem?

As Brooke was later to learn, there are two essential features of a champion networker. The first is desire. That presented no problem for Brooke. He possessed that first feature in abundance. Indeed, the desire to better himself was the only thing that kept Brooke going. His problem lay with the second feature. Brooke lacked that entirely. And that's what held him back.

What is the second feature? "The success thought process," says Richard Brooke, today president and CEO of Spokane, WA-based Oxyfresh USA. "The willingness to train yourself to think like a successful person."

Of course, most people lack the success thought process, initially. But Brooke, at first, had an even worse problem. He lacked the willingness to acquire the success thought process. And that will stop anyone dead in his tracks.

The first time Brooke was confronted with the science of motivation, he rebelled. In training sessions for the fuel additive company, Brooke's instructor urged him to write down his goals and to study motivational books like *Think and Grow Rich* by Napoleon Hill.

"If you read this book," his instructor promised, "and read other books like it and listen to tapes by successful people, you will begin to think the way they do. And once you start thinking those thoughts and believing those beliefs, you will become as successful as they."

"Baloney," thought Brooke.

Brooke "knew" that success had nothing to do with your thought process. Success came from getting straight A's in college and having a Rolodex filled with influential connections. Everyone knew that.

But he read the book anyway. At first, Brooke hated *Think and Grow Rich*. It might as well have been written in Greek. Brooke took over a year to slog through the slender volume, which many readers devour in a matter of days.

"It was difficult for me to read," says Brooke, "because the thoughts in the book were so contrary to my beliefs. I rejected them. That book and I were like repelling magnets, like water off a duck's back."

If only Brooke knew what he was rejecting!

In the early years of this century, the legendary steel mogul Andrew Carnegie had imparted to Napoleon Hill— at that time, a struggling young journalist—what Carnegie believed to be the secret of his success. Hill then spent the next 20 years interviewing over 500 other wealthy and successful men, including Theodore Roosevelt and Thomas Edison, in order to gain their secrets. The results of his epic survey were revealed in Hill's classic books, *The Law of Success* (1928) and *Think and Grow Rich* (1937). Hill had discovered that all great achievers build their success around a single, simple principle, which alone had the power to transform a pauper into a billionaire. But Brooke the chicken chopper didn't want to hear it. He thought he knew better.

Brooke might have gone through his whole life rejecting this life-giving information. But, as so often happens, he was saved by a personal crisis. Few things are more conducive to action than having your back to the wall. Brooke found that out the hard way. His greatest despair led to his ultimate salvation.

For the first three years of his network-marketing business, Brooke had relied for emotional support upon a man named Kurt Robb. Robb was the head sales trainer for Brooke's MLM company. Brooke idolized him. In training classes, he hung on Robb's every word, soaking up inspiration. When Brooke was down, Robb would always pick him back up.

"I saw him as my hope," says Brooke. "Having him around was my security blanket."

Then, one day, Robb was killed. A freak wave hit him on the beach in Hawaii. His head struck a rock and he drowned. Brooke was devastated.

"I realized then that I had a choice," said Brooke. "I could choose to quit because I'd lost my mentor. Or I could honor him by taking what he'd taught me and implementing it."

Until that point, Brooke had seen himself as a permanent student. He'd always put off actually using Robb's techniques, because he thought he still had more to learn. But now the teacher was gone. And there was no more excuse to wait. He decided, "If it's to be, it's up to me."

Brooke was completely on his own. Driven by fear and desperation, Brooke set to work mapping out his goals— something Robb had told him to do years ago. He started every day with a chapter of Napoleon Hill, or a bracing dose of some other motivational book or tape. He read *As a Man Thinketh* by James Allen, *Psycho-Cybernetics* by Maxwell Maltz, Og Mandino's *The Greatest Secret in the World,* and many more. All day long, Brooke would repeat positive phrases to himself, programming his subconscious mind to expect success. At night, he closed his eyes and visualized himself closing sales, recruiting top performers into his downline, and raking in scads of cool, hard cash.

At times, Brooke felt like an idiot. Was this really him? The perennial skeptic? The cynic? Was he really behaving like all those wacky "positive thinkers" he'd mocked and teased for so many years?

Yes, he was. And in no time at all, his new regimen began to bear fruit. Big fruit. He expressed his new philosophy this way: "The world has the habit of making room for the man whose words and actions show that he knows where he is going" [Napoleon Hill].

Brooke had learned the secret to success, that single, simple principle about which Napoleon Hill had written more than fifty years before. It was the power of goalsetting.

"Most people have goalsetting confused with desire," says Brooke, who today teaches seminars on positive thinking and writes books with titles like *Mach II with Your Hair on Fire: The Art of Self-Motivation.*

"People think that if you write down all the things that you desire, that's goalsetting. It's not."

According to Brooke, everyone is a goalsetter and a goal achiever, whether consciously or not. But your true goals are not necessarily the things you want. They are the things you expect.

When he was struggling to build his first downline, Brooke wanted to be rich and successful. But he expected to fail. That was his unconscious goal. And he "achieved" it again and again, much to his dismay.

"When I tried to recruit someone into my downline," says Brooke, "I'd say something like, 'Gee, I don't know if you'd be interested, but maybe you'd like to hear about this part-time opportunity. . . .'"

Deep down inside, Brooke didn't really believe that anybody in his right mind would sign up for his downline. And it showed. Brooke's recruits were few and far between. Most failed to excel and dropped out after a short time. Try as he might, Brooke could never manage to land the "Big Fish"—that top-level sales performer who would catapult his lucky sponsor to overnight riches.

But as Brooke began to take charge of his own daily thought process, to interrupt his negative thoughts as they appeared and to consciously evict them from his mind, something happened. His goals began to change. He began to expect success.

That's when Brooke met Jerry Schaub.

"I just went through the same sales routine I always did," remembers Brooke. "He looked at the business, and he said, 'I can do this. Just show me how.'"

Schaub was a tiger. Over the next year, he recruited hundreds of people into Brooke's downline. Brooke earned $100,000 in commissions from Schaub's sales in that one year alone.

Needless to say, Brooke's confidence soared. "I went out and found myself three or four more Jerry Schaub's in the next year."

Brooke had become a master recruiter. He wasn't using any new technique. He was selling the same opportunity he'd been pushing for four years. The only thing different was Brooke himself.

"Before, I was projecting too much doubt," says Brooke. "People sensed something was wrong, and they put me off. But now my energy level matched the words I was saying. People pay much more attention to who you're being than to what you're saying."

Brooke made his first million before he turned 30. He bought a $200,000 lakefront home in Orlando and a $40,000 Porsche. Today, at age 38, Brooke is president and majority shareholder of Oxyfresh USA, Inc., a $12 million network-marketing company in Spokane, WA, which sells toothpaste and other personal care products.

"There are no secrets to success," concludes Brooke. "The ideas have been around for centuries. All you have to do is use them."

The moral of the story? You don't have to be born with a positive attitude. As Richard Brooke proved through his remarkable metamorphosis, positive thinking is purely an acquired characteristic.

Trait #2: *Teachability*

The second trait of a Wave-Three networker is "teachability."

Many new recruits make the mistake of quitting before they've even mastered the basics. They fail to understand that network marketing is a profession that must be learned like any other. Past experience is nearly useless in network marketing. No matter how successful you were in your past career, you must listen to the instruction of your sponsor and stay with the program until you've learned the basics. As Mark Yarnell, Nu Skin distributor, says, "Every great network marketer was a lousy network marketer first."

"I've had my worst luck with people who were successful in previous careers," says Yarnell. "Instead of listening to their *upline* [those above them in the organization], they think they know everything."

Yarnell once recruited the president of an electronic parts factory. The man was a brilliant inventor and entrepreneur, with a gold mine of influential friends in the business community. But he knew nothing at all about network marketing.

"The first thing I told him was do not go out and prospect your most high-calibre friends and associates," says Yarnell. "I told him to wait until you've been trained and I've had a chance to work with you on your first few people in three-way meetings."

Three-way meetings are a keystone of Wave-Three network marketing. They make life easier for new recruits. All you have to do is bring your prospects to meet with your sponsor. The sponsor—in this case, Yarnell—does all the selling. You just watch and learn.

But the man disregarded Yarnell's instructions. Instead, he tried to do things the hard way. He went straight to his ten most successful friends and business associates and tried to recruit them on his own. The man knew so little about the business himself that he was unable to answer their obvious objections.

"When those friends told him he was an idiot, he believed them and decided he was in the wrong business," says Yarnell. "He didn't last 30 days."

Wave-Three networking is technically a lot easier than old-fashioned sales. But it requires more from a person's character. Without the humility to submit to your sponsor's training, no amount of high-tech distributor services or sophisticated management systems will ever bring you success. You must rely on the system and trust your sponsor's advice.

Trait #3: Generosity

"I believe that you can get anything in life you want if you will just help enough other people get what they want," says Zig Ziglar.

For thousands of years, sages have taught the Law of the Harvest as the surest route to success. It simply states that the farmer reaps more than he sows. As in agriculture, so in network marketing. The way to attain wealth is to give freely of your time, money, and compassion. When your growing downline clamors for help and attention at all hours of the night, only a warm and generous spirit will keep you from slamming down the phone in a rage.

Armstrong Williams used to take money out of his own pocket to buy products in the name of people in his downline, so they could qualify for higher commissions.

"I always made sure my downline knew they were not alone," says Williams. "I gave them a support system. I gave them my home number. I gave them my work number. I told them you can call me anytime, day or night. I told them you can set up meetings, and I will come by and do the demonstration for you. Because I never want you to feel that you're alone."

In keeping with the Law of the Harvest, Williams gained back from his downline far more than he ever gave. Not only did he earn $70,000 in his first six months, he built a life-long network of devoted friends and business associates.

Trait #4: Skin Like a Rhinoceros

As Wave Three takes hold in the economy, network marketing is enjoying a vastly improved image. Nevertheless, network marketers still need to brace themselves for a barrage of discouragement from friends and family. Many will still poke fun the minute you announce you've joined a network marketing company. Be prepared for the worst. Cultivate a hide as thick as rhinoceros skin. And always remember that criticism is the surest sign that you're making an impact. "There is a sure way to avoid criticism," said Napoleon Hill. "Be nothing and do nothing. Get a job as streetsweeper and kill off ambition. The remedy never fails."

When Tom Pinnock decided to abandon his writing career and concentrate on building his MLM business, his professional colleagues were aghast.

"I never figured you for a crook, Tom," said one editor at the daily newspaper where Pinnock had worked as a reporter.

"My father was shocked and disappointed," Pinnock remembers. "He was convinced that my sponsor was going to load me up with a garage full of products, and then go lickety-split across the Georgia state line with the police hot on his heels. Most of my family was that way, my in-laws, my brothers and sisters. No one could believe that this thing was real."

But Pinnock knew they were wrong. As a reporter, he'd made barely $30,000 per year, working 60 hours a week. He stayed out till all hours chasing stories and rushing to meet deadlines. Pinnock had become a stranger to his own children, who were asleep when he left in the morning and in bed when he returned at night.

"It was eating at me inside," says Pinnock. "I wanted to be my own boss. I just didn't want to answer to anybody else. I didn't want people telling me what I had to wear to work, when I could take my vacations and my lunch."

Finally, Pinnock took the plunge. He signed on as a distributor for Reliv, a new MLM company based in Chesterfield, MO, that sold nutritional supplements.

His gamble paid off in a spectacular way. Contrary to the snide insinuations of Pinnock's father and former colleagues, the business turned out to be not only perfectly legitimate, but extraordinarily lucrative.

Pinnock claims he made $100,000 in his first year—an unusually high first-year figure even for a champion networker. Pinnock's jeering relatives fell silent as they watched him put up a down-payment on a 3,300-square-foot home and a Mercedes SL sports car. They scratched their heads in disbelief as Pinnock flew off with his family on working vacations to Mexico, New Zealand, and other exotic locales, where Pinnock was building international downlines. On weekdays, when other fathers were hard at work, Pinnock was squiring his kids to the zoo.

"When they saw all that," says Pinnock, "they began to say, 'Hey, maybe Tom's smarter than we think he is.' "

Today, most of Pinnock's close relatives have joined his downline, including his father, who now supplements his retirement income with $2,000 per month from his Reliv business. Today, with a downline 20,000 strong, Pinnock pulls in about $700,000 per year.

"The criticism was very hurtful," Pinnock remembers. "When people don't believe in you, it makes you question yourself. I just had to separate myself from them. I didn't talk about the business around them. I had to go out there and prove that I was right."

Trait #5: Enthusiasm

Success in MLM comes only to those who burn with enthusiasm. You can't fake it. You must be genuinely proud of your work. If you're not excited about your network-marketing opportunity, how will you get anyone else excited?

"I've gotten to the point where I can tell right away if someone is going to work out in this business," says Mark Yarnell. "I just look at their level of enthusiasm. If a person calls me back the very next day after he's seen the program and says, 'Mark, I lost sleep last night just thinking about this. I'm so excited I can't stand it,' I guarantee I've found a potentially successful person."

You don't have to be a high-energy person to exude enthusiasm. You just need to believe in your product. Enthusiasm grows from your deepseated conviction that other people want and need what you're selling. And it fades when you know deep down inside that what you're selling is useless or overpriced. Choose a company with a great product, for a great price, and your energy level will take care of itself.

Trait #6: Drive

If you're looking for a way to "get rich quick," try investing in commodities. Network marketing is the wrong place for you. Most top networkers have gotten where they are through long, agonizing months of bone-crushing labor and sleepless nights.

Pat Newlin had always led a pampered life. Her husband, a prosperous attorney, had equipped her with the trappings of royalty. She lived in a 6,000-square-foot mansion with four acres of land, a private tennis court and stables, live-in servants, two Mercedes, and two private airplanes.

Then it all came to an end. Newlin's husband lost his fortune through bad business decisions. Their house burned down. Their marriage broke up. Suddenly, Newlin was on her own, a single mother with four hungry children.

"I had no money of my own," she recalls. "I had been a schoolteacher, but had not worked for 16 years. So I had absolutely no business experience. I literally do not know how to balance my checkbook to this day."

Newlin decided to try network marketing. She signed on with Reliv. From that moment, she worked around the clock. For various reasons, Newlin found a greater opportunity to build a business in California than her home in Austin. For months, she commuted from Texas to California, where her downline was growing rapidly. She spent one week in California for every week at home. Newlin's teenage daughter minded the other children while she was away. But Newlin felt guilty about neglecting her family.

"I had to sacrifice a lot of time with my children," she says. "I missed their back-to-school nights, their soccer games, their cheerleading. I couldn't be a Girl Scout or a Brownie leader anymore. But I was determined to make this work. I had to provide for my children. That's what kept me going."

Newlin reached her lowest moment six months after starting the business. Burglars broke into her home and stole everything. All her months of hard work seemed to have been for nothing.

"It was probably one of the worst moments of my life," says Newlin. "I was on the verge of cracking up. I was an emotional wreck. I had shingles. I cried all the time."

But Newlin found her salvation in hard work. Never slacking for an instant, she worked her business harder than ever. So absorbed did she become in her labor, that Newlin was almost startled when she got a call one day from Reliv headquarters.

"Congratulations," they told her. "You've made presidential director."

Newlin had hit $8,000 per month in commissions—qualifying her for the highest level attainable in the company. She had only been at it for eleven months.

"I've never been more excited and proud," she remembers. "I jumped up and down and screamed. It was something that I'd worked for. I worked harder than anybody else."

Today, Newlin makes over $100,000 per year. But even today, she has no intention of resting on her laurels. Newlin's goal is to make that much in a month.

"In over three years that I've been involved, I've never, ever quit working," she says. "I don't expect everybody to work as hard as I have or to make the sacrifices I've made, because they may not want what I want. But see, I want it all. And I know I can have it all."

Trait #7: Incredible Persistence

Many networkers claim that persistence is the critical factor in MLM success. All other traits can be learned or acquired, with time. But unless you persevere through every obstacle, neither hard work, positive attitude, thick skin, enthusiasm, generosity, nor teachability will have a chance to work their magic.

Richard Brooke is a case in point. For three years after becoming a fulltime network marketer, Brooke hung on by his teeth. He ended up begging money from relatives, running every credit card he had to the limit, selling his house, moving onto his sister's couch, and borrowing her car to get around. After three years, Brooke was $25,000 in debt and making about $4,000 per year. His family suggested as nicely as they could that maybe it was time to grow up and get a real job.

"I got a lot of pressure from my parents and sister," Brooke remembers. "They told me it wasn't working, that I shouldn't trust these MLM people, that I was spending money I didn't have."

But Brooke refused to give up.

"I just hung in there," he says. "I believed it would work. I'd seen it work for others."

It took three years of this torment before Brooke's ship came in. But, Brooke's dogged persistence was ultimately rewarded with fabulous wealth.

FOR LEADERS ONLY

If you're interested in network marketing just to make a small, part-time income, you can do it without the super-human qualities described in this chapter. But your chance to build phenomenal wealth depends upon your willingness to sacrifice. Think hard before deciding whether it's worth your while. It's one of the toughest decisions you are ever going to make.

Chapter 3

HOW TO SPOT A
WAVE-THREE COMPANY

"**J**erry, you're missing the boat. If you want to make money, you should get involved in multilevel marketing."

The year was 1983. Former '60s radical Jerry Rubin had become the toast of the New York nightclub scene, raking in more than $5,000 per week from his yuppie networking parties. He couldn't imagine how things could possibly get better. Not until a friend pulled Rubin aside one night at a party.

"Multilevel marketing?" said Rubin, echoing the words of millions of Americans in similar conversations. "What's that? Is that Amway?"

With a kindly chuckle, the friend explained to Rubin that he represented a new company that was getting ready to revolutionize the network-marketing industry. The company was well financed, said Rubin's friend. The owners were bigtime investors with Hollywood connections.

"He told me one of them lived next door to Johnny Carson in Beverly Hills," recalls Rubin. "The other owned the biggest office building in Los Angeles. He said they were going to professionalize MLM."

The man courted Rubin for days. He showed him slick, glossy brochures, expert medical testimony vouching for the products. He went over the numbers with Rubin, proving mathematically that he could make Rubin a rich man.

"I realized that this took all the same skills that I'd used as an activist in the '60s," says Rubin. "The '60s was about people-to-people networking. One person tells another person we're marching on the Pentagon, and then that person tells two people, who tell four people. I saw I could be good at this."

Rubin took the plunge. He sunk thousands of dollars and weeks worth of time into the new venture. And, as he expected, Rubin proved good at it. His network-marketing business took off. Thousands joined Rubin's downline.

"I had 200 people a night waiting in line to go to opportunity meetings in my office," he says.

Then disaster struck.

"The horse died on me," Rubin recalls. "One day the phone rang and the son of the owner called me up and said the company filed Chapter 11 today. And I looked around and saw a large $5,000 office, I saw thousands of people that I had brought into the business, I saw two closets full of powder and food and I got angry. I got furious. Not only did I lose $30,000 of my own money, but I lost my existing business because I had put it aside to do this other business."

Rubin went into a deep depression. Night after night, he tossed and turned without sleep, wondering how he could have been such a sucker.

What Went Wrong?

Many believe that horror stories like Rubin's prove that network marketing is for suckers. Certainly, that's what Rubin decided.

"The next three or four years," he says, "a lot of people called me up about MLM. Presidents of companies called, top distributors called. I just hung up on them."

But there's another side to Rubin's story. Ten years later, he went on to become one of the most visible network marketers in the country. Rubin has gone public on national TV talk shows and in leading newspapers advocating MLM as the salvation of America. He is also a frontline distributor for Life Extension International, based in Arlington, TX.

Obviously, network marketing itself wasn't the problem. So what was?

STABILITY OR NOVELTY?

Rubin had everything going for him. But he had chosen the wrong company. "There is no such thing as a great MLM company," says John Milton Fogg, editor of *Upline*. "Distributors are responsible for their own success. . . . The best the company can do is stay in business."

Unfortunately, over 85 percent of MLM companies go belly-up in the first five years, most of them in the first 18 months, according to Corey Augenstein, publisher of *Down-Line News*.

That's why more and more network marketers are learning to value stability over novelty. In the past, networkers leapfrogged from one company to another, trying to "catch the wave" of the next big up-and-comer. They feared that if they stayed with one company too long, its market would become saturated, and they would be unable to recruit new distributors. Newness or novelty was the most important quality they sought in a company.

But Wave Three has changed all that. The hottest companies today are those that employ technology, distributor services, and innovative management to ensure long-term growth and stability.

This new thinking is reflected in *Down-Line News'* ranking of the top network-marketing companies as of January 1994. Its "A List" includes such oldtimers as Watkins, Amway, Herbalife, Nu Skin and Shaklee.[1] Of the 34 top

---

1. Company names are given in this chapter, and in this entire book, for purposes of illustration only. The author does not personally endorse any particular company. Your own due diligence should be your only guide in selecting a network marketing opportunity.

companies ranked by *Down-Line News,* 15 are classified as "old" or "mature" by *MarketWave.*

"Generally, avoid startups," says *Down-Line News* publisher Corey Augenstein. "Why pay for someone else's learning curve?"

IN SEARCH OF THE WAVE-THREE COMPANY

Although he doesn't use the term "Wave Three," University of Illinois marketing professor Charles King recommends companies with many of the precise characteristics of a Wave-Three organization, among them, a well-developed distribution network, advanced distributor support, prospecting videos, training programs, and sophisticated programs for international expansion and product diversification.

All of that costs money—the kind of money that you're more likely to find in a mature company than a startup. King recommends choosing a company with "a track record . . . and financial stability." That narrows the field considerably. According to *Success* magazine, "Only a half-dozen MLM companies have topped the $500-million mark."

I'm with Dr. King. Choose a network-marketing company for its Wave-Three infrastructure, not for its novelty. This chapter will tell you how to do that.

INFINITE MOMENTUM

A company doesn't have to be new to be futuristic. Indeed, some of the hottest Wave-Three companies today started out as Wave One or Wave Two organizations. Now they use Wave-Three innovations to spark *infinite momentum—*

growth that just keeps on growing, long after the company has matured.

Take Amway. After 33 years in the business, you'd expect it to be as stagnant as the Dead Sea. But Amway's sales have more than doubled in the past three years. Part of the reason is its lightning expansion into more than 60 foreign markets. Part of it is the astonishing speed of its new product introduction, with Amway's state-of-the-art, robotized factories spewing out more than 400 different products, ranging from home technology to personal care. Amway's "department store" approach insures an ever-expanding market from its existing customer base.

Nu Skin International is also pushing for infinite momentum, through what Dr. King calls *divisional diversification*. That means starting an entirely new division with a separate product line. It's almost like letting your distributors join a new MLM company, but without losing the security of their established network. In addition to its traditional skin and hair care products, Nu Skin now sells its own line of vitamins, weight-loss and other nutritional products, and over-the-counter drugs.

As a result, *Success* magazine has painted Nu Skin as one of the hottest network-marketing companies in the business, publishing a whole series of articles touting Nu Skin's rapid growth and cutting-edge management. Not bad for an "over-the-hill" company founded in 1984.

Whom to Believe?

Sooner or later, whether you're an MLM "virgin" puzzling over your first prospecting video, or a 20-year veteran lying awake at night wondering whether it's time to "jump ship" from your present company, each and every network marketer finds himself pondering that loneliest of all questions: "Whom should I believe?"

Should you believe your sponsor? The one who keeps assuring you that his Company X is the best in the business? Or should you listen to that distributor down the street? The one who says Company X is saturated and urges you to get in on the ground floor of Company Y? Or should you believe the media, the politicians, and the attorneys general? According to them, every network-marketing company is a potential scam, and you're a fool to be in this business in the first place!

Whom to believe? Alas, there exists no magical database from which to draw authoritative answers to this question. However, you don't have to work blindly. There are tools, resources, and techniques galore to make the job easier. Follow the steps outlined in this chapter, and you'll learn to evaluate a company like the pros. In the end, there's no guarantee you'll make the right decision. But at least you'll make an informed one. And that puts you way ahead of the pack in this industry.

STEP #1: IGNORE THE HYPE . . . AND THE "UNHYPE"

"Listen, if you put Blake Roney on your cover, you're gonna end up with egg on your face," warned a mysterious caller to my office. "Nu Skin is finished. All the Nu Skin distributors are bailing out and going over to Company X. If you want to know where the action is, take a look at Company X."

The time was December 1991. The place was the Park Avenue offices of *Success* magazine. I had been assigned to edit *Success'* first cover story on network marketing. Trying to decide who to put on the cover proved one of the more daunting challenges of my journalistic career. It also taught me some important do's and don'ts about investigating network-marketing companies.

The first rule is, "Go by the facts—not the hype."

At that time, Blake Roney, founder of Nu Skin, seemed a likely choice to put on *Success'* cover. Nu Skin was, after all, one of the great success stories in MLM history. After five years, it had reached 1990 sales of $230 million. And the company predicted it would finish 1991 with an astonishing $500 million in sales. Industry insiders assured me that Nu Skin was a worthy subject for our article, as did Valerie Free, the writer assigned to the story.

But my colleagues in the media told a different tale. Within recent months, a hailstorm of articles and TV news shows had questioned the company's ethics, implying that it was a "pyramid scam." In state after state, attorneys general announced that they were investigating the company. Naturally, distributors from competing firms—like my mysterious caller from Company X—lost no time in jumping on the bandwagon.

My dilemma was similar to that facing a prospective distributor. Was Nu Skin really finished? Was all the bad press really true? Just like a prospective distributor, I had to sift through the hype and get at the facts.

STEP #2: EVALUATE THE PRODUCT

Before you sign on with any company, ask yourself, "Can I sell this product?"

Think carefully about this question. It's not the same as asking, "Will the product sell?" Just because you see *others* selling the product easily doesn't mean that *you* can.

"You must be passionate about the product," says Dr. Srikumar Rao, a leading authority on network marketing. "You must be enthusiastic and have an emotional attachment to it."

According to Rao, the best products for network marketing are those you can't find in a store. Health and beauty products are excellent, says Rao, because their appeal relies so heavily on personal perception and mystique.

"One company was selling a formula that was supposed to rejuvenate you," says Rao. "I tried the product for a month and nothing happened. But I talked to a number of other people who swore by it and said that it made their bursitis or arthritis vanish. That's what you're looking for, products that people swear do things like that. That's how you get a core of dedicated users."

However, Rao cautions distributors not to cross the fine line dividing mystique from improper medical claims. Truthful personal testimony is okay, as in, "This is what the product did for me." Promising others they will achieve the same results can get you in trouble.

Make sure that the company itself stays well within FDA guidelines with its product promotions, advises *Down-Line News* publisher Corey Augenstein.

Augenstein also advises prospective distributors to make sure the product isn't overpriced compared with similar items sold elsewhere. It's best if the company holds a patent or distribution monopoly on the product, although this is often not the case.

Product Power

In investigating Nu Skin International, one of the first things I discovered was that the company's phenomenal rise was driven almost entirely by the strength of its product.

Like other inventors, from Henry Ford to Bill Gates, Blake Roney started with a magnificent obsession to create a better product—in this case, a better skincare product. Starting at age 24, the penniless college graduate put together a few friends, a crazy idea, and $500 in cash to build one of the mightiest empires in skincare history.

All of the Good, None of the Bad

In the summer before he started law school, Roney worked odd sales jobs, while his wife, a student nurse, made sandwiches at a local Arby's. Money was tight. Roney knew he would have to endure many years of sacrifice before realizing his dream of business success.

But one day, his sister Nedra told him something that would change Roney's life. She offered the opinion that all those huge, glamorous, multimillion-dollar skincare companies were selling junk. Invent a skin cream that really works, said Nedra, and you'll be a rich man overnight.

That was hard for Roney to believe. But he did some research.

"There was no product on the market taking advantage of the technology," says Roney. "Most of them put in just a little bit of aloe vera, vitamin E or A. But the remainder was filler—mineral oil, beeswax, or other substances that can even harm or age skin."

"We made a list of everything known to be good for your skin, dozens of them," says Roney, "and then we listed those that were bad. Only the good ones went into our product. Our motto was 'All of the good, none of the bad, no matter the cost.' "

Sell the Vision

At first, Roney found little support for his idea.

"Ridiculous!" said the marketing professors he consulted. "That's not how you market skincare!"

"It's a cute idea, kid," said the factory owners he called, "but your formula will cost three times as much to manufacture as other skincare products. We're not interested. You're just going to lose your shirt."

But Roney kept calling. Using an 800-number directory to save on long-distance fees, he cold-called every chemical and cosmetics plant in the country. It took months of canvassing before he found anyone willing to listen. But finally he found a factory willing to make his unique formula.

Strength Through Adversity

The strength of Nu Skin's product carried it through every adversity. In the hands of its young, inexperienced managers, Nu Skin might have foundered before it ever left port. But the product itself kept the company afloat.

The first obstacle was a lack of money. The young partners—Roney, his sister, and Steven Lund, a young lawyer friend of Roney's—couldn't even afford to pay for their first factory shipment. But, from the moment their first distributors sampled the product, skyrocketing sales kept the company in business.

"We invited people into our homes," says Roney, "and told them they had to bring their own containers, and we'd spoon it out from the gallon containers. They'd come with Tic Tac containers or whatever, and we'd plop a spoonful into it. The first shipment was sold when it came in. Two hours later, we were out."

Roney says that he realized within those first few weeks that his product would be big. "All of a sudden we saw the gleam in their eyes," he says. "As soon as there were a dozen people who'd sampled the product and come back with fire in their eyes, I knew this was going to work."

That's when the roller coaster ride began.

"It was a nightmare," remembers Roney.

Word of mouth spread like lightning around the country. Calls poured in from hundreds of strangers in far-off states, angrily demanding shipments of product that Roney didn't have.

"Every time a factory order came in, it was already spoken for," says Roney. "I'd take angry phone calls all day long from distributors, trying to placate them."

Late at night, after the distributor meetings, Roney and his brother Brooke would send out packages of product, while another partner, Sandy Tillotson, fended off angry callers.

"We kind of had to bluff it," says Roney. "We had to look like we were more on top of things than we were."

The rag-tag band of entrepreneurs would hold meetings in restaurants so people wouldn't see they were operating out of a rented basement. They photocopied their brochures at Kinko's and sealed their product in surplus cosmetic jars, after cleaning off the old brand names with nail polish remover.

"Ninety-nine percent of MLM companies spike and disappear in eight months," says Roney. "For the first three years, I woke up every morning wondering if we would last another week."

So absorbed did they become in their tasks, they were taken off guard when the money started pouring in—$100,000 in wholesale revenues the first year.

Today, 10 years after its founding, Nu Skin has over 100,000 active distributors, 1,400 employees, a glass-walled, 10-story, 126,000-square-foot corporate headquarters, and a huge distribution center in Provo, Utah.

"What kept us hanging in there?" says Roney. "We just knew that we'd buy this product ourselves if someone walked up and showed it to us. Common sense told me if I wanted to use it, there's a bunch more who want to use it, too."

STEP #3: CHECK THE PUBLICITY TRAIL

Not every network-marketing company is big or famous enough to leave a "publicity trail" in the media. But it never hurts to check. In this Information Age, looking up press clips has become as easy as making a phone call or punching a few keys on your computer.

If you have a PC and a modem, you can subscribe to CompuServe, Dialogue, or Lexis/Nexis. If not, you can always call a service like Mead Data Central. They'll run a Lexis/Nexis search for you on the name of the company and of its founders and fax you the information within 24 hours or less. These services carry articles from most major newspapers and magazines. However, for *Wall Street Journal* clips, you have to use a special service called JournalFinder.

If you strike paydirt and find some articles on your target company, watch out. Use them for what they're worth, but don't accept what they say as gospel. For one thing, journalists can make mistakes. For another, magazines, newspapers, and TV networks are businesses like any other. Their clients are companies who advertise. And, as *MarketWave* publisher Leonard Clements so eloquently puts it, "It's not in the media's self-interest to promote an industry like network marketing, which doesn't use advertising."

STEP #4: CONSULT INDUSTRY WATCHDOGS

Often, it takes an insider to guide you through the labyrinth of gossip, rumor, and innuendo that conceal a network-marketing company's true worth. There are several prominent experts now competing (consciously or not) for the title of "Ralph Nader of Network Marketing." Among the best are Corey Augenstein, Kent Ponder, and Leonard Clements.

These people study network-marketing companies from the consumer's, that is the distributor's, point of view. They can unravel the mysteries of compensation plans, cut through the hype, reveal the hidden skeletons in the closet. Several publish their results in their own newsletters and magazines.

STEP #5: FIND THE SKELETONS

Experienced businesspeople always do their homework before entering any binding agreement. They check out potential clients or partners, using a host of standard tools and techniques. These same methods can be applied to investigating any network-marketing opportunity. They don't guarantee a successful partnership. But they increase your chances dramatically of ferreting out any serious, hidden skeletons that a company may be hiding.

"If you owned a video store," says Leonard Clements, publisher of *MarketWave,* "and a supplier offered you a great deal on 1,000 copies of *Ishtar,* which you agreed to sight-unseen, and later you found that you were only able to rent one of them, would you sue the supplier you bought them from? Sure, some would. But who's the one that should have read the reviews, talked to the critics, called other video stores, or just watched the movie first? Who's really responsible?"

Your first step should be to check on the company's financial soundness. Many growing network-marketing companies die because they're undercapitalized. They use the profits from today's sales to buy inventory, hoping they can cover all their payments to distributors out of next month's money. Sometimes they get away with it, if sales grow fast enough. But more often, this game of Russian roulette ends in Chapter 11 bankruptcy. Distributors start waiting longer and longer for their checks, as company executives stall, waiting for more sales to come in. Pretty soon, the whole house of cards collapses.

If you're looking at a public company, all you need to do is pull a Dun & Bradstreet report, or request an annual report from the company itself. Dun & Bradstreet is available only to subscribers, but your banker or lawyer can probably pull one for you for about $200.

Unfortunately, private companies don't have to divulge their balance sheets. But certain crucial indicators will provide clues as to their real financial strength.

Start with the state attorney general's office and the local Better Business Bureau. You can obtain from them a record of any past complaints against the company. Dr. Rao also suggests checking with the local Department of Consumer Affairs.

"Talk to them in three or four different states where the company has a large number of distributors," says Rao, "not just in the state where it's headquartered."

Don't forget to check with trade organizations. The two principle trade groups handling network marketing are the Direct Selling Association in Washington, D.C. and the Multilevel Marketing International Association (MLMIA) in Irvine, CA. They'll let you know if they've heard of any serious problems with the company.

Remember that even good companies may have many complaints on file. All you're worried about is whether the company has resolved those complaints.

Keep Complaints in Perspective

In 1986, the Austin Better Business Bureau received a rash of accusations against a certain mail-order computer company. It sounded like a classic rip-off scheme, with complaints running the gamut from delivery of faulty equipment to problems with returns and credits. The Texas Attorney General's office launched an investigation. Legal action was considered. But in the end, the government backed down, after the company agreed to clean up its act by instituting a one-year warranty, a toll-free number, and hiring more customer support staff.

"It did not appear to us to be a clear-cut pattern of deceptive trade practices," concluded Allision Hall of the

Texas Attorney General's office. "It was more like not having their business together. My impression was that the owners, their attorney, and such were just children. They are a really young bunch."

I became aware of this situation when I wrote a profile of this company for *Venture* magazine in 1987. The preliminary media search turned up all the skeletons. But wisely, my editor told me to disregard them. She said that such problems were typical of fast-growing companies started by young, inexperienced entrepreneurs.

The company? It was Dell Computer. When I wrote my profile, sales were a mere $75 million. In 1992, they had climbed to $2 billion. Not bad for a company started by a 19-year-old college student, selling computers from the back of his station wagon. Michael Dell now routinely appears on the covers of publications like *Business Week* and the *Wall Street Journal*. In fact, *Inc.* magazine named him Entrepreneur of the Year in 1991. And nobody's heard a peep from any attorneys general for the last seven years or so.

"When you grow from zero to $7 million in sales in a couple of months," explains Dell, "anything can happen and will."

Allow for Growing Pains

The example of Dell Computer taught me an important lesson in conducting due diligence—make allowances for a company's youth.

Back in 1991, careful investigation convinced me that Nu Skin was going through normal growing pains. Most of its bad press was caused by an indisciplined sales force. Distributors lured new recruits with unrealistic income claims or used hardsell tactics to "frontload" recruits with more inventory than they could afford. Nu Skin responded by tightening its discipline, liberalizing its return policy, and introducing a more generous compensation plan. Impressed by the company's reforms, five of six state attorneys general dropped their investigations while the *Success* story was still being written.

I decided then that Nu Skin's amazing story was well worth covering in *Success* magazine, and Blake Roney's visage worthy of display on the cover. Time has revealed the soundness of my judgment. After nine years in business, Nu Skin is still going strong—one of a handful of network-marketing companies which can boast of such longevity.

When investigating a company, you should never ignore such danger signs as lawsuits, rumors, and regulatory scrutiny. Check out every allegation. But remember that controversy is not only inevitable in a young, fast-growing company, it can be one of the surest hallmarks of success.

People Trail and Paper Trail

"Success in any investigation depends on the skillful interweaving of paper trail and people trail," says Dennis King, author of *Get the Facts on Anyone.*

The "paper trail" of an MLM company consists of financial and legal records. The "people trail" consists of suppliers, distributors, company officers, lawyers, bankers, and accountants.

Start on the paper trail by getting a credit report (for instance from the TRW credit reporting agency) on the company. Ask your banker to help you. Some banks will even furnish a credit report as a courtesy to depositors. Look for late payments to suppliers. You can also call suppliers directly to see if the company is considered a reliable customer.

Next, you should ask the company for the names and phone numbers of its attorney, banker, and accountant. If the company has nothing to hide, it will grant this request without fuss.

Call the banker first. Ask whether the company is a borrowing customer, and if so, is it timely in its payments? Has it applied for credit, and was it granted or turned down?

"Ask the company accountant whether the company is having financial problems," suggests Rao. "Of course, he'll never run down his client. But will he give a ringing endorsement, or just say it's okay?"

Rao suggests requesting a P & L statement from the company's accountant.

"Nine times out of ten, he'll say no," says Rao, "but what have you got to lose? At the very least, your phone call will give you a chance to ask point blank whether the company has something to hide. You never know. He just might tell you."

Do the same with the company's attorney.

"Ask the attorney how long he's represented the company," says Rao. "Then ask whether the company was a plaintiff or defendant in any litigation and how much litigation has there been against the company?

"If the attorney doesn't divulge anything, try asking point-blank whether his client has something to hide. Listen closely to his answer. Small nuances can reveal a lot."

Luckily, you are not dependent on the company's lawyer for this information. You can obtain a litigation history for $60 to $80 from Prentice Hall Legal and Financial Service (to contact this company call (800) 221-0770). The search must be done in the county in which the company is domiciled. It will show you which court of jurisdiction heard the case and the type of crime, whether criminal or civil.

"A lot of small stuff not on the credit report will turn up here," says Rao, "like the guy who supplied flowers for annual meetings and never got paid. Look for a pattern of abuse."

Now check the judgments. Have there been any decisions handed down? For what and how much? Are there any state or federal tax liens?

The credit report will also note past judgments or lawsuits.

"When you check the litigation history," advises Rao, "be sure to do the same for the individuals who founded the company."

All of this will end up costing you several hundred dollars and a lot of your time. It's up to you to decide how thorough you wish to make your investigation.

A somewhat easier and cheaper method might be to contact a firm called CIC in Tampa, FL, which provides quick background checks on people for private investigators. Contact Bruce Berg: (813) 878-0198. A check on business credit will run you $36, personal credit check $12.50, criminal record $25, education $12, license verification $16, and prior employment $10.

Of course, many are comfortable relying upon a few references and a large measure of intuition. That's all right, too, if you want to take the risk. But remember Corey Augenstein's warning:

"Going into opportunity meetings or talking on the phone, you ask a lot of these questions," says Augenstein, "and they just don't have the answers."

STEP #6: EVALUATE THE SUPPORT SYSTEM

What makes network marketing work is the division of labor between distributor and parent company. A good company takes care of everything except selling and recruiting. Those are your jobs. If you find yourself fussing and fuming over things like product deliveries or, God forbid, overdue commission checks that means your company is not providing adequate support.

A Wave-Three organization, by definition, is one which employs substantial money, effort, ingenuity, and state-of-the-art technology to make this division of labor as clean as

possible. Only a few cutting-edge companies come close to
the ideal described below. But, with the Wave-Three revolution proceeding at a rapid pace, it will not be long before
this ideal becomes the standard.

To gauge a company's level of distributor support, ask
these questions:

Telecommunications

- Does the company provide a **three-way calling
  service**, at advantageous rates, for use in working
  with your upline or downline on sales, prospecting,
  and training? (See Chapter 7 for a discussion of
  three-way calling.)
- Does it provide a **voice-mail service** to distributors, accessible through an **800 number**? Voice
  mail greatly enhances your ability to communicate
  with your downline and prospects. (See Chapter 8
  for a discussion of voice mail.)
- Does the company's voice-mail service allow you to
  do **group broadcasts**?
- Does the voice-mail service give you **voice processing** capability (that is, the ability to do quick scans,
  to save certain messages while erasing others, to
  pause, repeat, or forward messages to other people)?
- Does it provide **satellite broadcasts** for sales,
  training, and prospecting?

Management Support:

- Does the company maintain an **information hot-
  line** to answer distributors' questions about product and other organizational issues? This is

necessary not only for your own personal information, but for your downline, so they don't have to bug you every time they have a question.

- Does it provide other information important for managing your downline, such as **updated genealogies** and **group sales volume**, by fax or voice mail?

Product Fulfillment:

- Does the company **fulfill product orders** from your downline and retail customers? If you have to do it yourself, you'll find yourself running a warehouse, instead of a network-marketing business. A Wave-Three company will take all the problems of order fulfillment—including credit-card processing, sales tax, and product returns—out of your hands.

- Does it provide an **800 number** that your downline and retail customers can use for ordering?

- Does the company offer an **automated delivery service**? Nu Skin's Automatic Delivery Program (A.D.P.), for example, will place monthly orders of those products you use most, saving you the trouble of constantly reordering.

- Can you order **one unit of the product at a time**, if that's all you need? Or do you have to buy a certain minimum amount?

- Does the company accept **credit card orders** by phone? **Personal checks**?

- Can you **order product 24 hours a day**?

- **How quickly does the company fulfill orders?** All product should leave the warehouses within 24-48 hours after the order comes in. You should also have the option to have it shipped by Fed-Ex or other overnight service, if you're willing to pick up the freight charge.

- Does the company provide immediate **confirmation of orders** by fax or voice mail?

Sales/Marketing Support:

- Does the company provide **teleconferences or satellite conferences** for prospecting and training? (See Chapter 7.)
- Does it provide **prospecting videos**, audio cassettes, and other marketing materials that help you to sell the opportunity?
- Does it **sell such materials cheaply**? The price should be at cost or close to cost. The company shouldn't be in the business of selling marketing materials. If you buy in bulk, audio cassettes should cost no more than $2, videos no more than $7.
- Does the company provide **tracking reports** of your customers' buying habits?

Training:

- Does the company provide **training programs** for distributors? How often? Are they free? Are they available in nearby regions and cities?
- Are such training and motivational seminars available through **voice mail** or **satellite broadcast**?
- Does it have **newsletters**, **video magazines**, or other **internal communications** to keep distributors informed?

International Expansion:

- Does the company have an **international expansion program**, allowing distributors to build

downlines in foreign countries, without the hassle
of taxes, licenses, and currency conversion?

STEP #7: EVALUATE THE COMPENSATION PLAN

In network marketing, the *marketing plan* or *compensation plan* refers to the manner in which a distributor is
compensated for his or her efforts. Usually, a distributor
draws income from four different sources: *(1) retail profits,*
which is money earned from selling product directly to customers; *(2) wholesale profits,* which is money earned from
selling product to distributors in your downline; *(3) overrides,* which is a percentage of wholesale profits paid to you
from those "legs" of your downline who have broken away
(see Appendix for a full explanation of "breakaway" plans);
and *(4) bonuses.*

Before choosing a company, ask yourself a few questions about the marketing plan. First, does the spread between wholesale and retail price give you an adequate
profit for your retail sales? Also, does the spread between
the wholesale discount you get from your upline and the
discounts you give to your distributors ensure you an adequate wholesale profit?

Second, does the company have breakaways? Is the
breakaway plan advantageous?

With a few spectacular exceptions, most compensation
plans in MLM pay out about the same once you break
down all the numbers. The main thing you have to look out
for is any evidence of *frontloading.* That means any sort of
requirement built into the plan that pressures you to
spend huge amounts of money loading up on product. This
is a more complicated issue than is usually acknowledged
in network marketing literature. See Appendix for a full
discussion of compensation plans and their various pitfalls
and strengths.

STEP #8: CONSIDER THE COMPANY'S GROWTH PHASE

As mentioned earlier, a company's phase in the growth cycle
was once the prime criterion by which many networkers selected an opportunity. But Wave Three has changed all that.

For one thing, the user-friendly revolution has opened
up the business to millions of new prospects. Companies no
longer have to fight so hungrily over the same, stagnant
pool of chronic MLM junkies. Wave-Three companies target professionals, small business owners, and other virgin
game. So a company need no longer be considered saturated simply because the junky caravan has moved on to
the next mirage.

In fact, as Leonard Clements of *MarketWave* points
out, the market for MLM prospects today consists potentially of every able-bodied man or woman in America—if
not the world. Experts estimate there may be as many as
6–7 million distributors in the United States today. That
leaves over 250 million Americans who've never even tried
it, people who are prime prospects for the new, user-
friendly style of network marketing. A Wave-Three company cannot truly be saturated until it has exhausted that
huge, untapped market.

Another development is a new perspective on the
growth cycle itself. Traditionally, networkers have seen a
company going through four distinct phases of growth,
which marketing professor Charles King has named, the
formulation phase, the *concentration* phase, the *momentum* phase, and the *stability* phase.

As you can see from fig. 3.1, the phase of most rapid
growth is the momentum phase—which occurs after the
company has exceeded $50 million in sales. This is the mo-
ment when exponential growth kicks in, when fortunes can
be made overnight by those lucky few who got into the company just before it went into momentum.

But Wave-Three distributors have become far more
aware of the dark side of momentum growth. They've become aware of an additional growth phase, falling some-

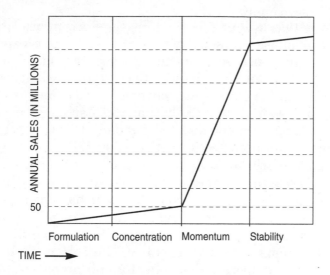

FIG. 3.1: THE FOUR GROWTH STAGES OF AN MLM COMPANY

where between Dr. King's momentum and stability phases. Leonard Clements calls it the *scrutiny* phase.

That's the phase when the regulators and attorneys general start noticing the new kid on the block. That's when government bureaucrats start casting covetous eyes on fat corporate bank accounts, dreaming of all the fines they can impose. That's when investigations start and the bad press hits.

Amway, Herbalife, A.L. Williams, Nu Skin—all the big boys have gone through the scrutiny phase and put it behind them. They've jumped through the fiery hoops and lived to tell about it. Those who have survived the scrutiny phase form a very short list.

"If I had to pick a stage as most optimum," says Leonard Clements, "I would say six months prior to the onset of momentum, in a company that will last at least the next 30 years. But that's a little like saying that the best time to invest in a public company is just before the price goes up. No one can predict it."

In network marketing, as in the stock market, you simply must ask yourself whether you're a high-risk speculator or a no-nonsense blue-chip investor. Obviously, you're going to make out like a bandit if you somehow manage to spot the next Nu Skin or Amway just before its momentum phase. But it's far more likely that you'll spend year after year jumping from one doomed company to another, until you finally quit network marketing altogether.

Can you still make money in a big, established company? Of course. As long as it's a Wave-Three organization—a serious, long-term company that has developed a host of strategies for ensuring steady, predictable growth by constantly expanding its product lines and using advanced systems and technology to create easy methods for distributors to operate domestically and abroad. And as long as you don't mind making your money slowly and patiently, with a lot of hard work.

"There's going to be a big blowout in the '90s," says Augenstein. "Only the strongest, the best run, the best managed, the best products, the best compensation plans will survive."

Blue chip or crap shoot? Ultimately, the choice is yours.

Get the Facts

Aristotle Onassis wrote that, "the secret of business is to know something that nobody else knows."

That's as true in network marketing as in any other industry. But knowledge doesn't drop from trees like Newton's apple. You must go after it. The price of knowledge is long hours of painstaking research. Believe no rumors. Ignore the press. Shut your ears to know-it-all friends and colleagues. Get the facts.

Someday soon, they'll all be scratching their heads and wondering how you made such a "lucky" guess.

SECTION 2

ORGANIZATION

Chapter 4

THE SEVEN DEADLY PITFALLS
OF BEGINNERS

L et's say you just signed up for a network-marketing opportunity. You've compiled your "warm list"—a roster of all the people you know on a first-name basis. You close yourself in your study. You reach for the phone to start calling.

And you stop dead.

"I don't know what to say," you gasp in horror. "I need a recruiting script!"

So you call your sponsor and pick her brain for an hour. You consult a couple of how-to books and listen over and over to an audiotape on recruiting pitches. Several days later, you reach once again for the phone. You start punching in a number. Your hand freezes in midkeystroke.

"But what if my prospect says no?" you think. "I need to know how to handle his objections."

So you call your sponsor again. She gives you some pithy comebacks for the most common objections. You write all your scripts out carefully and lay them in front of you, arranging them alternately in different patterns. Then you reach once more for the phone.

"Wait a minute!" cries a little voice inside. "What if my prospect asks for a detailed description of the compensation plan? Does the company have a video to explain it? I'd better call my sponsor . . ."

GETTING STARTED: THE ULTIMATE HURDLE

"Nothing will ever be attempted," said Samuel Johnson, "if all possible objections must first be overcome."

The single biggest hurdle in network marketing is getting started. Procrastination stops many recruits dead in their tracks before they make their first phone call. Discouragement decimates those who remain. By the time their first year is over, up to 90 percent of MLM recruits have simply quit.

"I've had people quit after 30 days, and tell me, 'I'm sorry, but I gave it everything,'" says Mark Yarnell. "But how can you give it everything in 30 days? In 30 days, you haven't even learned how to overcome objections. I've gotten to the point where, if a person won't make a one-year commitment, I refuse to sign them up."

Why do so many aspiring networkers drop out before they've even properly started? In most cases, it's because they've succumbed to one or more of the Seven Deadly Pitfalls of Beginners—a motley array of misconceptions, time wasters, and flawed strategies guaranteed to nip any successful MLM business in the bud.

Simply avoiding these seven perils will put your fledgling business at a considerable competitive advantage. They are as follows.

Pitfall #1: Reinventing the Wheel

"There are three things people need to know to do the business," opines Doris Wood, president of the Multilevel Marketing International Association (MLMIA). "One is how to sell, one is how to sponsor, and one is how to train the people you've sponsored to sell, sponsor, and train."

At its root, network marketing is a simple process. The simpler you keep it, the closer you stay to your real objectives. Nevertheless, inexperienced distributors are always seeking ways to make the business more complicated. Instead of following the tried-and-true procedures taught by their sponsors, they waste precious time and energy trying to reinvent the wheel.

New distributors are often disappointed to discover that network marketing takes a lot of hard work. They fall victim to *gimmick-mania*—an obsessive search for clever shortcuts or gimmicks that they hope will minimize their work while maximizing their commissions. Such schemes never succeed. Gimmick-mania leads inexorably to disappointment and defeat.

A prominent third-world diplomat was once inducted into Nu Skin distributor Mark Yarnell's downline. He seemed like a dream recruit. "The guy had more high-level connections than anybody else I ever signed up," says Yarnell. "He was teaching at a major university. He was known to three presidents. He drove around in a limousine in Washington, D.C. He was a major international businessman and an ambassador."

But the diplomat soon revealed himself as an incurable gimmick-maniac.

"He never did anything," says Yarnell. "He never signed up one person. He was always coming up with a new scheme and a new system to help him make a million dollars a year without applying himself."

Yarnell urged the diplomat to hit the streets and start selling, sponsoring, and training. But the man thought he had a better idea. He proposed turning the juiciest phone numbers and contacts from his Rolodex over to Yarnell and his downline, and letting *them* do all the work! To the diplomat, it seemed an ingenious system—combining his contacts with other people's sweat. But in network marketing, "Everybody's got to carry their own load," says Yarnell.

Unable to lower himself to retail, recruit, and sponsor like the other peasants, the diplomat finally dropped out after only four months.

Few networking neophytes are quite so full of themselves as this international wheeler-dealer. But most are tempted to overcomplicate the business, in one way or another. One of the most dangerous temptations for beginners also seems the most harmless—*technomania,* the irrational urge to invest in high-tech hardware.

Of course, Wave Three itself is made possible by technology. Fax broadcasting, voice mail, and teleconferencing allow distributors to communicate cheaply and efficiently with downlines tens of thousands strong. Computers let you design your own ads, publish in-house newsletters, or spew out thousands of labels for mass mailings right from your desktop. Recruiting videos let you pitch your opportunity to hundreds of people at once in as many different cities.

But in the Wave-Three organization, the safest place for technology is in the hands of the parent company. Computers at the home office relieve distributors of distractions like calculating commissions, fulfilling product orders, and keeping track of their downlines. Wave-Three infrastructure should free distributors, as much as possible, from the need for personal computing power. For in the unsupervised hands of distributors themselves, technology often becomes one of the most fatal distractions of all.

"Technology is just another excuse for not making cold calls," says Mark Yarnell. "I'm computer illiterate. My idea of a filing system is the yellow legal pad that I keep under my bed upstairs. I don't know how to do a computer. I can't type. I don't even know how to work a word processor or a Wizard. It's unnecessary, because this is a business where you sit in your living room in blue jeans and talk to people about making their lives work."

An unhealthy obsession with gadgets, gizmos, and "systems" often masks a fatal pattern of avoidance. For most people, face-to-face selling is a terrifying prospect. Endless tinkering provides a seductive alternative. In extreme cases, the syndrome progresses until you've purchased thousands of dollars worth of audiovisual aids, high-tech office equipment, and computer hardware. In the final stages, you spend a fortune on newspaper ads and purchase mailing lists and software for addressing envelopes. Direct mail, after all, is the surest way to avoid talking to another human being.

When Tom and Terry Hill first started working together on their Nu Skin business, they tried to keep track of every sales lead on a personal computer. As a stockbroker for Merrill-Lynch, Tom had been accustomed to keeping such files on his clients, and so had Terry as a saleswoman for Xerox. But the longer they worked their business, the less need the Hills seemed to have for detailed record-keeping.

"It was just a time waster," says Terry. "We would sit there for hours and hours putting prospects in the database."

One day, the Hills decided to give their PC away to the Salvation Army. They've never regretted it. Today, they manage their global downline of over 5,000 people without so much as a fax machine. On those rare occasions when they must send a fax, they use the service down the street.

"Your phone is the most important thing," says Tom. "You couldn't live without the phone. Any records I keep I just put them on index cards."

The Wave-Three office is a minimal office. When Kathy Denison started her Nu Skin business, she set up a workspace in her bedroom with nothing more than a desk, a phone, and some shelves to store product samples.

Because Denison was still working full time as a maid when she started her business, she made a decision to set aside one full hour each day to work on network marketing. "I didn't go to bed at night unless I had done my hour," she says. During that hour, Denison confined herself ruthlessly to selling.

"If I didn't have someone coming over to the house," she says, "I would call people and set up appointments. I would work on my warm list. I did action. There's only two things to do in this business, and that's sell the products and talk about the business opportunity. So if I wasn't doing those, no matter how much I was preparing in my house, doing book work, setting up my office, I wasn't really getting anywhere."

Denison's stripped-down approach served her well. She rose from a lowly maid to a millionairess in just a few years.

Despite stories like those of Denison and the Hills, expert opinions continue to proliferate on how to make network marketing more "sophisticated." Some advise ambitious distributors to rent an office, fill it with fax machines, secretaries, and computers, then show up every day at 9 A.M. in a suit. Others argue that this "professional" approach defeats the main purpose of MLM, which they say should enable ordinary people to work from their homes and keep a flexible schedule.

Regardless of where you stand in the debate over "professionalism," there is no denying that network marketing is based on person-to-person interaction. No matter how many hours you spend staring at a computer screen, sitting at a desk, or shuffling through papers, you'll never get the job done. You've got to make cold calls and sponsor people. It may not sound glamorous, but it's the method that works. Any other system you devise is just reinventing the wheel.

"People will always choose the path of least exposure if they can get away with it," says Terry Hill. "It's human nature. But this is a belly-to-belly business. You have to get out in front of people and talk to them."

Pitfall #2: A Small-time Attitude

"At the very beginning, I had a very clear picture of what the company would look like when it was finally done.... I realized that for IBM to become a great company it would have to act like a great company long before it ever became one."

—Tom Watson
Founder of IBM

Many network marketers fail because they treat their businesses like hobbies or part-time jobs. They dabble, rather than commit. Most simply lose interest in the business after a short time. Others lose control of their business as soon as it starts growing. Promising opportunities dissolve in a tempest of chaotic files, poor planning, and faulty priorities.

To make it big, you have to think big—right from day one. That means implementing procedures, policies and systems appropriate for a multinational corporation—and sticking to them. Even if you're the only one on the payroll.

"My success was largely due to the fact that I had my back against the wall financially," says Mark Yarnell. "I didn't have the luxury of treating my business like a part-time job. I had to treat it like Big Business."

Yarnell structured his workday as if he were a Fortune 500 CEO. From 6 to 8 A.M., he planned his day and programmed himself with motivational books and tapes. At 8:30, he got in his car and drove downtown, where, for the next hour, Yarnell approached professionals on their way to work and handed out business cards.

Promptly at 10 A.M., Yarnell arrived back home for a scheduled meeting with anywhere from five to ten prospects in his living room. He always made sure they were out by 11:30 A.M., so Yarnell could spend the next 30 minutes calling the people he'd met that morning and scheduling further appointments.

After lunch, Yarnell held another meeting, then hit the streets once more by 4 P.M.

"I literally had structured five days a week from 6 A.M. until 8 in the evening," says Yarnell. "I treated it as if it were a legitimate business."

In his first 90 days, Yarnell recruited 89 people. "I signed up one a day for the first three months. And I signed up a total of 311 frontline distributors in my seven years."

Pitfall #3: Making Yourself the Issue

"You don't want people to base their perception of the business on what you personally have or haven't done."

—Howard Solomon
Quorum, Diamond Executive

When you start out in network marketing, you're usually a poor advertisement for your company. Your cash flow may be negative. You're angry, frustrated, and discouraged much of the time. You don't have ready answers for the tough questions your prospects ask. In that condition, you're more likely to scare away prospects than entice them. What can you do?

Track upline.

That means find a successful person in the levels above you who is willing to act as your mentor. Then use that person as the lure for new prospects.

Mark Yarnell was a sad specimen when he signed on with Nu Skin. For ten years, he'd worked as a preacher in a little country church. But when the Texas oil and real estate markets fell through, Yarnell's weekly contributions dried to a trickle. His personal salary plunged below $800 per month. The bank repossessed his car. His house payments fell two months behind.

"We were starving," Yarnell remembers. "We were in big, big trouble."

For the first few months of his Nu Skin business, Yarnell's cash flow was hardly an inspiration to his downline.

"My second month in the business, I made $217," he says, "and I probably spent $800 on long-distance phone calls."

When prospects came to Yarnell's house, he tried to downplay his poverty. Yarnell would hide his beat-up old Chevrolet in his neighbor's driveway, so visitors wouldn't notice the cracked windshield and the two missing hubcaps. But, being a man of the cloth and a law-abiding citizen, Yarnell could hardly lie about his income.

"In your first four to six months," says Yarnell, "you need to be able to say to a person, 'I just got started, and I'm not making any money, but my coach is making $50,000 a month, and here's his personal phone number. Call him.' "

Unfortunately, Yarnell's sponsor—the man who recruited him into the business—was just as ineffectual as he.

"My sponsor had signed up the day before I did," says Yarnell, "so he didn't know anything. I tracked upline. I called *his* sponsor and *he* didn't know anything either. He'd only been in a month or two. I just kept calling and asking, 'Who's your sponsor?' till finally I got through to Richard Kall. Richard was making a lot of money, so I knew he knew what he was doing. I called him up in Long Island and said, 'I'm willing to do whatever you teach me.' "

From then on, Yarnell followed Kall's every word of advice. He phoned Kall when he was discouraged, plied him with questions when he was puzzled. When Yarnell found a good prospect, he set up three-way conference calls with his mentor, listening quietly and taking notes while Kall made the presentation and closed the sale.

In conventional businesses, most people shy away from seeking a mentor. They imagine that busy, successful people have no time for them. But in network marketing, your upline has a financial interest in helping you. Even if you are so far down in the levels of your mentor's organization that he draws no commissions from your volume, you're still a good investment for him. Your mentor knows that a real go-getter will eventually exceed the volume of the people above him, and will "roll up" quickly through the levels.

Thus, Mark Yarnell is today directly in Richard Kall's frontline . . . even though he was six levels below Kall when he made that first phone call.

Pitfall #4: *Taking Rejection Personally*

Whether you prospect by phone, direct mail, TV infomercial, or computer bulletin board, you will ultimately be compelled in your network-marketing business to meet new people, by phone or face to face, and pitch them on your opportunity. Many will say no. Novices all too often take such rejections personally. They immediately blame themselves or the opportunity. But the successful network marketer understands that the problem is usually nothing more than timing.

"My experience has shown that if people are at the right time in their lives, they're going to get involved in this business no matter how it's presented," says Mark Yarnell. "Conversely, if the timing isn't right in their lives, I don't care how brilliant, skillful, and articulate you are. They're not going to get involved."

Armed with this realization, top networkers learn early to slough off rejection and move on to the next prospect. As top network marketing trainer John Kalench puts it, "SW, SW, SW—Next!" That stands for "Some will, some won't, so what—next!"

Some rejections are worse than others. Reliv distributors Kirby and Cynthia Wright probably experienced one of the worst forms of rejection there is—*mass* rejection! When they threw a big opportunity meeting at a hotel, no one showed up.

After holding their first hotel meeting, the Wrights thought they'd discovered the key to easy wealth. Between the Wrights and their ten part-time distributors, they managed to get 57 people to attend.

"It was a good feeling," remembers Cynthia. "We signed up three or four frontlines that night. It felt like we were on our way now."

The Wrights scheduled a hotel meeting for the following month, expecting to double or triple their attendance. But when the time came to start the presentation, they realized the only guest in the room was the 17-year-old niece of one of their distributors. And she wasn't even a real guest. She had just come along with her aunt for the ride. And only seven of their distributors had shown up.

In a brief moment of panic, the Wrights toyed with the idea of cancelling the meeting. But the words of their up-line sponsor came back to haunt them.

"Our sponsor always told us you've just got to do it," says Wright, "that it doesn't matter if anybody comes or not, you've just got to be set up and you've got to do it."

As if walking in her sleep, Cynthia mounted the podium and opened the meeting. At first, the eight people in the audience seemed perplexed and uncertain what to do. But after Cynthia cracked a few jokes about the sparse attendance, they warmed up and got into the spirit of the game. Soon, they were cheering and applauding as if they had a thousand people in the room.

"We needed the practice anyway," remembers Cynthia. "Everyone needed to hear the presentation again. And it turned out okay. Everyone there had guests who didn't show up, and we all needed a lift. The meeting got people excited again. We left that night ready to start the day to-morrow, to call up people and ask them why they weren't there."

The Wrights were saved by their faith in the system. In a trying moment, they had relied on their sponsor's in-structions, even when every bone in their body cried out to abandon ship.

Had the Wrights lost their nerve and cancelled the meeting, it's likely they would never have attempted an-other one. Instead, they went on to build a six-figure in-come for themselves and to later hold meeting after meeting with attendance figures in the thousands.

Of course, most network marketers will never be re-sponsible for such large hotel meetings, nor will they expe-rience such massive rejection. But the principle that sustained the Wrights in that trying moment remains the same whether you're throwing a small home party or just meeting with a single prospect. Rejection is always devastating. It can stop you in your tracks. But strict adherence to the rules and procedures taught by your sponsor is the surest way to build inner confidence and to find the strength to move on to the next challenge.

"The presenter's only real responsibility is to show this opportunity to as many people as they possibly can every day for one to three years," says Yarnell. "If they do that, the numbers will take care of themselves."

Pitfall #5: Neglecting Your Retail Sales

In their rush to recruit a big organization, many network marketers disdain selling product at retail. "Let your downline do the selling," they say. But your downline will take their cue from you. If you don't sell, they won't either.

In truth, there is only one way to make money in network marketing—moving product. Unlike franchises, MLM companies are forbidden by law from earning profits through the sale of distributorships. And, in most states, MLM companies are required to buy back any product that their distributors can't sell. Thus, every penny that moves through a network-marketing company must come ultimately from selling product at retail.

Of course, that doesn't mean a network marketer must become a salesperson for life. As you grow more successful, you'll probably choose to delegate more and more of the selling to others. But in the first months of your business, you should apply yourself personally to building retail sales. This accomplishes two important objectives. First, it prepares you to teach others how to sell your product. Second, it provides an immediate income stream during those early months when your downline is producing little or no commissions or overrides.

While building his downline, the impoverished Yarnell had to lay out a lot of money in order to keep up appearances for his prospects. A wealthy parishioner loaned him money to decorate his living room with rented furniture, lease a big-screen TV and stereo system, and even rent a new car. But Yarnell paid his monthly bills largely through his income from retailing Nu Skin products.

" I had people coming to my house five, six, seven times a day to pick up their products," says Yarnell, "After my first month, I was selling enough product that I caught up on my car payment. I had my house payment caught up by the end of my third month."

It wasn't until months later that Yarnell finally received a substantial commission check for thousands of dollars. But during those lean early months, his retail business had seen him over the hump, providing up to 43 percent of his monthly expenses.

Pitfall #6: *Listening to the Dream Stealers*

"You should never engage other people in a discussion about our industry," says Mark Yarnell, "until you're fully trained and confident and ready."

If you do, you might succumb to the "dream stealers." These might be close relatives, professional colleagues, or virtually anyone you know and respect who tries to impose their dim view of network marketing on you. Mistrust of the industry is the number one cause of attrition among new recruits, according to experienced networkers. Unless you wish to become one of those statistics, you've got to ignore the dream stealers, and give the business a chance to prove itself.

Bill Elsberg made a big mistake when he took his newlywed wife Sandy to an opportunity meeting in Phoenix, AZ. Cynical New Yorker that she was, Sandy glared with contempt at the speaker's plaid polyester pants and gum-soled shoes. She winced when he promised the audience they could earn $28,000 per month working part time.

"You wanna buy the Brooklyn Bridge?" Sandy asked her "naive" Midwestern husband afterwards. "If you believe this guy, you'll believe anything."

Like so many well-meaning spouses, Sandy was playing dream stealer. Opposition from loved ones has caused many people to abandon network marketing before they even began. But Bill pleaded with his wife to give him a chance. "Just give me six months," he said. "If it doesn't work, I'm out."

Sandy granted the six months. But she didn't make them easy. Bill worked around the clock, seven days a week, maintaining a full-time job as a colon health practitioner, and spending nights and weekends on his network-marketing business.

"When I would go to bed at night, he still wouldn't be home," Sandy remembers.

Sandy shared her concerns with her father. When Bill's first check came in for only one hundred dollars, the old man exploded. "He's got a girlfriend," said Sandy's father. "Why would somebody work 30 days and 30 nights for just one hundred dollars? Get a rental car and follow him."

But Sandy withheld judgment just a bit longer. The second month, Bill earned $300. The month after that, he brought home $500."

"I said, 'Bill, you're killing this relationship,'" Sandy remembers. "We're never together. We don't go out. This business isn't working." But Bill stayed the course. By the sixth month, his income had climbed to $3,800 per month.

From that point on, Sandy ceased being a dream stealer. More than that, she went on to become a full-time networker herself, even supporting Bill when a debilitating illness forced him to give up working for an extended time. Today Bill and Sandy are successful distributors for Life Extension International. But they would never have made it had Bill not shut his ears to the dream stealers and given his network-marketing business a full six months to prove itself.

Of course, the best defense against dream stealers is education. Do your homework. Read up on the industry. Familiarize yourself with the innate strengths of network marketing. Then you can fight back against the dream stealers with cold, hard facts.

"People need to understand," says Quorum distributor Howard Solomon, "that it is immaterial whether they like our industry, whether they feel comfortable with our industry, or even whether they get involved with it. Network marketing's time has come and there's nothing any of us can do to alter the course of history."

Pitfall #7: Abusing Your Sponsor

Your sponsor is your most crucial resource. He's there to advise you, encourage you, assist you in selling and recruiting. Lose your sponsor's good will, and you've cut off your life line.

Too many networking neophytes burn out their sponsors with endless complaints, lamentations, and other emotional demands. They treat their sponsors as psychotherapists—a role for which most successful distributors have neither time, training, patience, nor stomach.

Mark Yarnell got in the habit of crying on his sponsor's shoulder when things went wrong. After four months of laboriously building his downline, seven of Yarnell's frontline executives jumped ship to another company. In a state of paralyzing depression, Yarnell called his sponsor, Richard Kall.

"He just said, 'Quit being a sissy and go to work. You're wasting all your time worrying about people you've lost. You ought to be out getting new blood.'"

Many times during his first year, Yarnell threatened to quit. Instead of pleading with him to stay, his sponsor would call his bluff.

"He was never sweet and loving," Yarnell remembers. "He would just say, 'You're right, Mark, you don't have what it takes. Don't bother me anymore.' That type of thing. I hung up on him many times. There were times when I got off the phone and I swore I'd never call him again."

But Yarnell stuck with it. Indeed, he learned a key lesson from those painful conversations. He learned that there was really nothing his sponsor could do to resolve his complaints, short of working his business for him. By shrugging off Yarnell's self-pitying pleas, Kall pumped him full of exactly the fuel he needed to succeed—an angry determination to prove himself.

"He was a real slave driver," says Yarnell. "But it was powerful. It was effective. It was what I needed. I needed somebody to reflect back the truth, and the truth was that I was being fearful and making excuses."

Sandy Elsberg prides herself on being a "nurturing" sponsor. Ordinarily, she eschews the harsh "take-it-or-leave-it" approach of a Richard Kall or a Mark Yarnell.

"I'm a gardener, not a hunter," says Elsberg. "My usual way of sponsoring is nurturing, caring, praising, and motivating."

Nevertheless, when a recruit takes her too much for granted, even a mother hen like Elsberg is sometimes forced to get tough with her "chicks."

Elsberg once recruited a former Catholic monk named Daniel Bushnell. Bushnell couldn't seem to pull his life together. His dirt-poor rural upbringing and his monks vows had left him with what Elsberg calls a deep-seated "poverty consciousness." But Bushnell wanted to change. He was desperate to overcome his fear of making money.

"Daniel told me he wanted to earn $2,000 per month," Elsberg remembers, "and he said he would put in whatever time it took, and do whatever it took and whatever I said in order to get there."

But ten months later, Bushnell was still treading water. He wouldn't work the plan. He wouldn't commit to regular hours. He wouldn't accept challenges from Elsberg to accelerate his retailing and recruiting. As a result, Bushnell was pulling in barely $200 per month.

"For ten months," says Elsberg, "Daniel didn't pay attention, didn't commit, and didn't honor our faith. He wasn't producing, he wasn't taking direction, and he wasn't following the plan."

One New Year's Eve, as Elsberg sat drawing up her goals for the year, she was suddenly moved to call Bushnell.

"I told him that I thought he was a phenomenal human being and that I wanted to stay friends with him for life but that, as a business associate, he was terrible and that I didn't want him involved with my business," says Elsberg. "Just before I hung up, I asked him, 'By the way, what did you get your mother for Christmas?' "

At first, Bushnell resented Elsberg's "tough love."

"He told me later that he was angry," she says. "He despised me at the moment. But he called me up the next day and said, 'I'm ready to go to work.' "

Today, Bushnell is one of Elsberg's top producers. And he teaches his own recruits according to Elsberg's philosophy of "tough love."

"I want to help my downline as much as I can," says Bushnell, "but it's easy to end up handholding and babysitting them instead. I believe we sponsors can best lead by example, by keeping our fire intact, our conviction and commitment level high. A sponsor should be a warrior, a leader, and a conqueror, not a den mother."

STRENGTH AND WEAKNESS

Wave Three, with all its systems and technology, will never eliminate the danger of these Seven Deadly Pitfalls. They reflect the essence of human strength and weakness, the delicate balance upon which your network-marketing business will succeed or fail.

Rely on the system, yes. But rely on it only to create fresh opportunities to exert yourself to the maximum. The Wave-Three attitude requires that you test your endurance every day. Make no excuses. Delay no decisions. Never let a day pass unproductively. Only then will the intricate synergy of the Wave-Three infrastructure come mysteriously to your aid.

Chapter 5

WAVE-THREE SELLING

"**D**on't you ever talk to me about Nu Skin again!" said the woman angrily. "If you do, I will not be your friend anymore. I'm sick of hearing about it."

Kathy Denison was devastated. She had suffered the salesperson's worst nightmare—a *nasty* rejection. And from someone she liked and respected!

Denison loved talking about her business and products. It was an obsession. Indeed, ever since Denison had become a Nu Skin distributor, she'd followed the "three-foot rule." That meant everyone within a three-foot radius was fair game for a sales pitch. More than once, Denison had sprung the tactic on this woman in her aerobics class. But now Denison was afraid she'd stepped over the line.

"I never spoke to her about Nu Skin again," says Denison. "I didn't want to be in people's face to the point where nobody could be around me."

MOST PEOPLE HATE SELLING

"Take a little test," advises John Fogg, editor of *Upline*. "Ask yourself how many people will you talk to who will turn you down for your product . . . before you quit? The

91

truth is that the number is startlingly small for most people. It's somewhere between 3 and 10."

Let's face it. Most people hate selling. They hate it because selling exposes them to the constant threat of rejection.

In the book *Learned Optimism,* John Creedon, president of Metropolitan Life, is quoted as saying that his company only selects 5,000 out of the 60,000 applicants for sales positions each year. Half of those quit in the first year. Those who remain sell less and less every year. After four years, 80 percent are gone. Indeed, according to Creedon, 50 percent of all insurance salespeople in the entire industry quit every year.

"Selling is not easy," Creedon concludes." It's an unusual person who can do it well and stick with it."

Why does Creedon lose so many salespeople? Rejection, he says.

"Every single day," he explains, "even the best agent has quite a few people who say no, usually a number of them right in a row. . . . Once the agents get discouraged, they take the no's harder and harder; it takes more and more effort for them to get up and make the next call."

Finally, they just stop trying.

If hardened sales professionals suffer such devastating attrition, how can network marketers, coming as they do from all professions and walks of life, possibly survive?

The answer is that most of them don't. Or, at least, they haven't, up till now.

Wave-Three Selling

But network marketing is changing. Advanced Wave-Three organizations have refined and perfected the selling process in such a way as to insulate networkers from the worst impact of rejection. Such companies also provide a built-in system for replenishing self-esteem, which puts to shame the most expensive corporate incentive and training programs.

This new form of selling amplifies the strengths of ordinary people, rather than exposing them to their worst fears. It promises, in coming years, to redefine the very concept of salesmanship.

I call it *Wave-Three selling.*

Network Power

Wave-Three selling takes the pressure off the individual and puts it on the network. Of course, no system, no matter how sophisticated, will ever quite remove the sting of rejection. Nor will it guarantee a sale for every pitch. But the Wave-Three organization provides an infrastructure of technical, human, and emotional support uniquely engineered to bring out the best in the individual salesperson. Like a gigantic echo chamber, the network amplifies the efforts of the individual many times over.

On her own, Denison had no hope of selling anything to the angry woman in her aerobics class. Nor did she try. She did what any normal person would do. She backed down and never talked about Nu Skin to the woman again.

Nevertheless, two years later, Denison received a surprise phone call.

"I want to get into your Nu Skin business," said a familiar voice. It was the woman from the aerobics class!

The reluctant prospect had been won over with no effort at all on Denison's part. She had simply been absorbed into Denison's network. Long after Denison left the town of Aspen, CO, where they had met, the woman continued to feel the power of Denison's growing network all around her.

Everywhere she went in Aspen, Denison's distributors and customers seemed to surround the woman. Mutual friends kept her abreast of Denison's growing success and of Denison's happy new life in California. When she visited

local friends the woman spied Nu Skin products ordered
through Denison in many of their bathrooms. Ultimately,
she could no longer resist the aura of glamor and success
now radiating from Denison's downline like a magnetic
field. She wanted to be part of the group, part of the excitement.

Customers for Life

When you sell by absorption, you make customers for life.
A prospect, once integrated into your network, has every
reason to stay in it, and very little motivation to leave.

The woman from Denison's aerobics class originally
signed up as a distributor. But, like most recruits, she
didn't remain active in the business for long. She became
instead a regular wholesale buyer of the product. To this
day, she remains one of Denison's most faithful customers.

Build Customer Networks

Wave-Three sellers build *customer networks*. They recruit
into their downlines masses of people who buy products at
wholesale for themselves and their families, but have no
interest in acting as distributors.

"About 70 percent of my personal group consists of
wholesale buyers," says Denison. "You want as many people as possible to be wholesale buyers in your organization."

Only in network marketing does every product carry
with it an invitation to a new way of life. Conventional
salespeople spice up their offers with discounts, rebates,
warranties, and service contracts. But network marketers
offer their customers a gateway to the future.

THE TOTAL SALES CULTURE

By joining a network, Wave Three customers gain early access to the primary distribution channel of the 21st century. They join the *total sales culture.*

In the future, as network marketing spreads to every industry and point of the globe, its interlocking matrices of customers and distributors will mesh together so thoroughly as to become indistinguishable. A distributor for one company will also be a registered wholesale buyer for half a dozen more. And vice versa.

Selling will become a normal adjunct of everyday conversation. Let's say your neighbor expresses an interest in buying a certain drain cleaner you recommended. You simply provide him with your personal identification number. He uses that number to order the product via an interactive home shopping network. By using your PIN number for the order, your neighbor alerts the company that it should send you a small commission on the sale—a commission which you'll continue to get every time he buys that product in the future!

Sales Charisma, Not Sales Science

In recent years, corporate sales staff have come to behave more and more like scientists. Salespeople today study more Freud than do psychotherapists. They manipulate prospects' choices through neurolinguistic programming. They craft intricate forecasts using math that would befuddle an Einstein. On today's corporate sales forces, you find an array of specialists rivaling the crew of a NASA control room—prospectors to set up deals, negotiators to dicker over contracts, and closing specialists to sign them.

Does all this specialization sell more widgets? Nobody knows. But one thing is clear. Network marketers will have none of it. As the years go by, networkers seem to have, if anything, less time, less inclination, and less need to jump on the bandwagon of scientific selling.

Why?

Because, in the Wave-Three organization the network itself handles all the science. Videocassettes present sales pitches crafted by professionals. Product demonstrations are scripted down to the last detail. Distribution is handled electronically, through automated, toll-free numbers. Given a good product, every sales member in a Wave-Three company operates on the same, level playing field.

"We have a 15–20-minute program of crime prevention demonstrations," says Quorum distributor Howard Solomon, whose company sells security devices. "It's all on video, it's all on audio, or you can just read it, memorize it, whatever. It's wonderful. It works very effectively. A lot of retail is being done because of that program."

With every technical variable thus minimized, only one arena remains in which the Wave-Three salesperson must excel—the arena of personal charisma. In the Wave-Three organization, a networker's aura of personal influence will radiate through downlines and customer networks like conductable energy. Customers will adhere to your network as much because of who you are as what you are selling.

Filled with the Spirit

"The essence of charisma is showing your commitment to an idea or goal," wrote communications guru Roger Ailes in *Success* magazine.

No one could have shown a clearer commitment to any goal than did Kathy Denison. From the time she was a small girl, Denison knew exactly what she wanted.

"I wanted to be a millionaire," she says.

Denison spent most of her life with her nose pressed against the glass, peering in on the secret world of the superwealthy. With its world-famous ski resorts and exclusive neighborhoods, Aspen, CO was a playground for movie stars and millionaires. Denison discovered that she could get close to the rich by serving them.

After getting a job managing Aspen's most exclusive women's clothing store, Denison met many of the city's leading socialites and was even invited to parties at their homes. But Denison never forgot who she was. She was a single mother, with a daughter to support. And she was so poor that she had to wear the same clothes to work day after day.

"I was always the worker, and they were always the women out skiing every day and shopping and buying the most expensive clothes and flying into Palm Springs and having face lifts and all of that," says Denison. "I wasn't envious, but it made me aware. It opened up my mind to a different way to live."

The Selling Grid

Left unchecked, the raging waters of Niagara Falls are a wild, destructive force. Only when passed through hydroelectric turbines and filtered through a "power grid" of transformers and high-voltage lines are Niagara's deadly rapids reduced to fuel for living room lamps.

In like manner, the charisma of Wave-Three sellers could never move a single product in and of itself. Only when channeled through the *selling grid*—that invisible network of systems, procedures, human interactions, and telecommunications that comprise the Wave-Three organization—can their unruly passions be sublimated into useful effort.

The Forces of Chaos

Kathy Denison's hunger for success made her a fireball of energy and activity. From the time she rolled into Aspen at age 26, her baby daughter and all her possessions in her car, Denison was afire with ambition. In her desperate struggle to excel as both mother and breadwinner, Denison could somehow manage to do neither. She leapt from one career to another. Denison roofed homes, finished furniture, painted houses. She dabbled in a succession of cottage industries, from making collages for restaurant decorations to selling arrangements of wildflowers she picked in the woods. Denison even tried selling her own skincare potions, made from oils and herbs she bought in health food stores, sealed in little hand-painted jars.

But all this furious activity never seemed to pay the bills. Denison couldn't feed her daughter without food stamps. In the end, she abandoned each new business venture in despair, reverting back to full-time work, leaving her growing daughter alone much of the time.

Denison's energy was as boundless as Niagara's thundering rapids. But without an orderly channel through which to flow, her torrential outpouring of hard work and business ideas dissipated into mist.

The Linear Trap

The problem was that Denison was no entrepreneur. She was a small business person. And the only thing she could accomplish with all her plans and schemes was to create more linear work for herself—work, which, by its nature, would always fail to make enough money for her.

The Outward Reflects the Inward

Because she failed to recognize the essential problem, Denison's life continued to unwind. For a while, she sought haven in marriage. But five years with her ne'er-do-well husband left her worse off than when she started. In the end, Denison had to flee with her daughter, under a police protection order, to avoid her husband's drunken rages.

"After that marriage, I had very low self-esteem," says Denison.

But she had a worse problem than that. While still married, Denison and her husband had started a cleaning business. It sounded very entrepreneurial on the surface. But as Denison trudged from door to door hawking her services, she couldn't help feeling that she was something less than a "business owner." Her skin broke out from the cleaning chemicals she used. Many of the affluent Aspen homes she cleaned were the same in which she had once socialized.

"It was incredibly humiliating," Denison remembers.

Often, when Denison was on her knees scrubbing a bathroom floor, she would hear guests arriving and recognize the voices of friends and acquaintances, or even famous movie stars dropping in.

"I just looked at myself and thought, God, I know I can do better than this," says Denison. "What am I doing here? Why am I cleaning houses and they're out skiing every day? What is the difference between them and me? Why am I the worker and they're the players?"

Inner Order

In fact, the answer to Denison's question was very simple. She lacked inner order. To impose the order of a functioning business on the wild chaos of the marketplace is the task of a giant or a genius. Those who possess this talent become great industrialists and entrepreneurs. But most people need guidance. They need someone else to tame the marketplace for them. They need someone else to impose the order that they lack within.

Each day, Denison felt her illusion of "business ownership" slipping further and further away. At age 43, she was a maid, not an entrepreneur. She labored every day on her knees, scrubbing other people's toilets.

Desperately, she explored the idea of becoming a real-estate broker. It required no startup capital, and one could ultimately make a lot of money at it. But deep in her heart, Denison knew it would just degenerate into one more debilitating distraction. It meant learning one more product, one more entirely different way of selling, one more business she would have to frantically learn while caring for her daughter and cleaning homes, and she knew ultimately that it, too, would soon dissolve into chaos and failure.

Friends urged her to franchise her cleaning business, but Denison couldn't think how to reduce her daily drudgery into a system that others would want to buy.

Slowly, it began to dawn on Denison that she just couldn't do it on her own. She needed a system of someone else's devising, an orderly structure through which she could channel her energies.

"I didn't want to be 50 years old cleaning houses," says Denison, "and so I asked God for a financial opportunity. I said just send me something, because all my life I've wanted to be a millionaire."

RETAIL OR WHOLESALE? THE ULTIMATE SALES PITCH

One day, Denison got a call about a new client who had just moved into the exclusive community of Snowmass. Reluctantly, Denison dragged herself to work.

"I had an attitude I didn't really want to be there," she recalls.

But that cleaning job was destined to change her life. The new tenants were Nu Skin distributors. When she came in, Denison noticed boxes of skincare products lying all over the house. From her own dabbling in the skincare business, Denison knew from the ingredients that they were of unusually high quality. "I asked the man who lived there where he got the products," says Denison, "and he said, 'We're in network distribution.'"

Denison's cleaning client, Mark Yarnell, then made Denison the ultimate sales pitch.

"You can buy them from me at retail," he said, "or you can become a distributor and buy them wholesale. Whichever you prefer."

The Fusion Sale

Network marketers often speak about "separating" their retail sales efforts from their prospecting for recruits. But, in practice, the two endeavors work best when done in tandem. In that first meeting with Yarnell, Denison, like most practicing network marketers, was won over by the *fusion sell*—sometimes called the *recruit-to-sell* approach.

Had Yarnell simply offered the products at retail, Denison might have bought on the spot. But their relatively high price might also have kept her from coming back. Yarnell would have achieved a one-time sale, but would have failed to build up his customer network.

But when Denison was offered a choice between retail and wholesale, her brain started going a mile a minute.

"I knew that my friends would be interested in buying these products too," she remembers, "so I thought I might as well become a distributor and get them wholesale, because then I could turn my friends on to that."

SELL THE DREAM

Even if your prospect has expressed no interest in anything except the product, it doesn't hurt at the very first meeting to let her know about The Dream. Just so she can think about it. What dream? The dream of financial freedom, of course.

"Well, since you want to become a distributor," said Yarnell, upon hearing her reply, "I want to show you something."

Yarnell disappeared into his bedroom and came out with a monthly commission check for $15,000.

"This is what I made with this company last month," he smiled.

"I was in shock," says Denison. "I couldn't believe it. The most money I had ever made was $4,000 a month. I said, 'My God, how did you do that?' "[1]

LET THE TOOLS DO THE SELLING

Wave-Three organizations provide a wealth of selling tools—videos, audiotapes, and written material—expertly designed to do your selling for you. The more you rely on those tools, the more time you have for targeting other prospects. Videos are best. A well-produced prospecting video gives authority to your product and your opportunity. It can present your product, your compensation plan, and the very concept of network marketing effectively and engagingly within 30 minutes. You probably can't.

The moment Denison asked how he made so much money, Yarnell knew she was hooked. But instead of answering her question and spending the rest of the afternoon talking to her, Yarnell said,

"I don't have time to explain it right now. Why don't you take this video tape home and look at it and see what you think?"

---

1. This conversation took place in 1988, before growing legal controversy over income claims made it risky for prospectors to show checks. This author sees no moral or ethical objection to making accurate income claims. But neither Mark Yarnell nor any other distributor or company cited in this book recommends showing checks in today's legal environment.

The Multiplier Effect

One video can affect an entire family or a group of friends, in the same time that it would take you to personally give a sales pitch to just one person.

In Denison's case, because she didn't have a VCR at home, she took Yarnell's videotape to a friend's house, and the two of them watched it together. Later, Denison watched the same tape with her daughter. Before she returned that tape to Yarnell, it had converted three people, not just one.

SELL THE NETWORK

No fusion sell is complete unless you also sell the network.

That means selling not only the product or the opportunity, but also the convenience and support of buying or working through that particular company.

As you're selling, your prospect is watching you carefully to see how hard it is to work this business. If you spend three hours explaining the product or the opportunity, most prospects will start calculating in their heads how many three-hour slots they have in the course of a week for such sales marathons.

But if all you do is hand them a video, they think, "Hey, that's easy. And it only takes a few minutes for each person. I can do this too!"

After viewing Yarnell's video, Denison suddenly understood what had been missing in her previous business ventures. It was the power of the network—a system designed by others wiser and more experienced than she. But one in which her own unique gifts would be magnified by the power of duplication.

"When I saw the technique of creating an organization five by five (referring to the standard MLM technique of recruiting five leaders who go on to recruit five leaders apiece, and so on)," she says, "I knew that I could do this business, and I knew that this was my opportunity to finally achieve my goals and dreams financially."

Other selling features of the network might be your company's drop-shipping program, such as Nu Skin's Retail Advantage or Reliv's Direct Select. You can also talk about the future of network selling through interactive TV, and about specific programs your company is planning to introduce.

Push Till They Push Back

If you push too hard, you may lose customers who would otherwise stay in your network for years. Learn to be sensitive to the signals people send you. If you sense they are pushing back, stop pushing.

"After they had bought products from me for a while," says Denison, "I offered the distributorship to everyone. And a lot of people just said, 'Hey, I don't want to. I just want you to service me.'"

GET 20 CUSTOMERS FIRST

The technique of fusion selling makes it virtually impossible to target customers independently from your recruiting prospects. Nevertheless, when you begin your selling, it is a good discipline to set a goal of finding 20 retail customers before recruiting a single distributor.

You need a retail customer base so you can keep moving product downward. Otherwise, you will be tempted to stockpile product in order to keep your monthly wholesale volume up. Some companies actually forbid distributors to buy product at wholesale unless they have moved a certain amount at retail each month. Denison recommends building up a personal retail volume of $500 to $1,000 a month before turning your efforts to recruiting.

Selling at retail will also force you to become intimate with the product and will build your confidence that it's something people really want.

"You get to know what you're selling," says Denison. "And you start to believe. You know what you're talking about—you know what the products are about—because you're using them and selling them to people, and you're seeing some results."

BE A PRODUCT OF THE PRODUCT

"Network-marketing companies for the most part have products that the consumer doesn't yet recognize that he or she needs or wants," says Howard Solomon of Quorum. "And so it's up to the independent distributor to make the consumer aware that the products exist and that there's a viable need for them."

Until the total sales culture goes on line, it will require a hefty cultural leap for people to buy something from a network marketer, rather than a store. They won't do it without some compelling reason. And the most compelling reason of all is that you have something utterly unique that they can't get anywhere else.

The best way to get this message across is to become yourself a "living demonstration of the product." Use the product yourself, and don't even presume to go out and sell it unless you've attained such beneficial effects that you can vouch in all sincerity for its value. If you are yourself a true believer, that is the most engaging sales pitch of all.

Denison's first big catch came as a direct result of her personal use of the Nu Skin products. One of her cleaning clients was a plastic surgeon. As Denison cleaned his house one day, the surgeon remarked that her skin looked different. That was all the opening Denison needed. She launched into a full-fledged fusion sell.

"I told him that I was in this new business," she says, "and I was really excited about it. It was kind of hard for me to come from being a maid to telling a plastic surgeon I'm going to be a multimillionaire."

But she did it. That same day, Denison drove home and fetched her product samples and prospecting video for the man to see.

"He just looked at the products, looked at the ingredients and he said 'I'm in,'" remembers Denison. One month later, the surgeon filed his letter of intent with Nu Skin to become a breakaway executive.

"He jumped right into it," Denison enthuses.

Don't Sell—Demonstrate

More potent than your personal testimony is the customer's own five senses. Whenever possible, you should sell by demonstration, rather than persuasion.

Denison would bring clients to her house or make house-calls to give them actual treatments with the products she was selling.

"I just went through the normal routine of cleansing, exfoliating, moisturizing, and then have them lie down for 20 minutes for a facelift treatment," she says. "Anybody that tries that facelift will buy the product—it's incredible."

"And the skincare is so different than those products you buy in the department stores, you can feel the difference in your skin right away . . . that's how I got my clients."

Sell by Conviction

One of the most powerful weapons in the arsenal of a Wave-Three seller is the life-changing power of the opportunity itself. Just as a customer's interest in the product can be used to recruit that customer as a distributor, so a customer's interest in your business can be used to sell product.

When she first started her business, Denison simply announced to every one of her cleaning clients that she would no longer be available as a maid after the ski season ended in May—five months later.

"I'd say, 'After that, I'm done. I'm going into a new business,'" says Denison. "And they'd go, 'Oh my God, what are you getting into?' And I'd tell them that I had a whole new product line that I was introducing, and a lot of them said, 'Hey, come on over and show me your products.'"

Of course, Denison's tactic was risky. She had no guarantee at all that she would be financially independent in five months, or even that the company would still exist. But Denison believes her willingness to burn her bridges made a lasting impression on many of her clients, sparking their interest in the products.

"In order to be successful, you have to be 100 percent committed," says Denison. "You have to burn your bridges."

THE THREE-FOOT RULE

Your unique ability to reach people in your personal sphere of influence comprises your chief value to a network-marketing company. It's also your most potent selling advantage.

Many new distributors dither for months over which of their friends, relatives, and associates to approach and which not to. This kind of thinking can rapidly degenerate into complete paralysis. The best way to cut through it is to employ the "three-foot rule." That means you sell your product or opportunity to anybody who comes within three feet of you.

"I was pretty much the kind of person that only wanted to talk about the business," recalls Denison. "I was obsessive, compulsive . . . and I think you have to be obsessed."

Within the first couple of months, Denison had ripped through her immediate family and cleaning clients. She then fanned out to Aspen's professional community.

"I got a lot of people on the products," she remembers. "I got a lady who owns one of the big gyms in town. I brought in a lady that was a real-estate broker. I retailed a lot of products to my cleaning clients, too."

The principle danger of the three-foot approach is that it maximizes your exposure to rejection. Some warn that it may antagonize people and cause them to avoid socializing with you. But Denison ignored the negative reactions.

"Some people wouldn't listen because of who I was," she remembers. "I was cleaning houses, and they couldn't quite get the idea that I was going to be a multimillionaire. Some of them laughed at me. But some people are open-minded enough to appreciate somebody with a dream."

CUSTOMER SERVICE, THE KEY TO REPEAT SALES

In his book *The E-Myth*, management consultant Michael E. Gerber tells how he once tried out a new barber. The man washed his hair and cut it with scissors, while an assistant kept his coffee cup filled. Gerber liked the service and went back a second time. But this time, the barber used both scissors and electric shears, and did not wash Gerber's hair. Gerber's coffee cup was filled once, but not a second time. After a third appointment, in which the routine was changed yet again, Gerber decided he'd had enough.

"Something in me decided not to go back," writes Gerber. "It certainly wasn't the haircut—he did an excellent job. It wasn't the barber. He was pleasant, affable, seemed to know his business. It was something more essential than that. There was absolutely no consistency to the experience."

As Gerber demonstrates with this story, the real difference between a multibillion-dollar restaurant chain like McDonald's and the dingy Greek diner on the corner is that you know what to expect from McDonald's. Consistency is the key to customer service.

The ultimate in consistency is provided by Wave-Three services like Reliv's Direct Select, which allows retail customers to order through an 800 number and receive their shipment within days.

Nevertheless, even with such a high degree of systematization, the opportunity to provide additional service through one's own creativity and personal contact never disappears. For some customers it is these extras outside the Wave-Three infrastructure that make all the difference between staying in the network or leaving it.

Denison, for example, has retail customers from her early days who still refuse to go on the Retail Advantage program.

"I still have customers in Colorado that I have to mail stuff to," says Denison. "They don't even want to be on Retail Advantage . . . they want me to contact them, because they love the service. Retail Advantage is so much easier for me and them. But they want me to call up every month and say 'Hi,' and see how they're doing. They like the personal contact . . . when you have a lot of energy, people like to talk to you. So I guess I'm an energy source for them."

Build a Referral Network

It's a big mistake to try to build a customer network solely from your personal contacts. The savvy Wave-Three seller multiplies his contacts by building a referral network.

Whenever you add a customer to your network, try to obtain from him the names of other people he knows who might be interested in buying the product. Some networkers suggest asking each customer outright for ten names. But that can be off-putting. Some customers might be annoyed.

Denison used her referral network to penetrate the inner sanctum of Aspen's elite—people whom she may not have reached through her own social circles.

"Some of my customers in my cleaning business were in with the 'Who's Who' kind of people in Aspen," she says. "And so I made sure that I showed them the products and they had a good experience. Aspen is a small town, and everybody knows everybody. So you have to get in with the in crowd so to speak. The in crowd has to like something, if you want it to be popular."

Denison's high-class referral network enabled her to go after a husband and wife who owned one of Aspen's most exclusive stores. They were a big catch, enabling Denison to influence a far wider circle of movers and shakers.

"People looked up to them," Denison explains, "and so once they were in the business, people said 'I guess it's okay for us to look at it.'"

Through one of her frontline executives, Denison gained a referral to an owner of one of the top beauty salons in town. Today, the husband and wife team are regular wholesale buyers.

Dealing with Objections

Of course, not everyone will jump on the bandwagon. Many will say no. And if you allow them, they will undermine your confidence.

Early on in her business, Denison approached one of her cleaning clients, a woman whom she greatly admired. Married to a wealthy businessman, the woman epitomized the sort of jet-setting life to which Denison aspired.

"I looked up to her," says Denison. "I wanted to be like her, travelling all over the world, having the best clothes, a beautiful home, working out every day, president of this, president of that . . ."

But when Denison showed her the products, the woman turned up her nose.

"She had sort of a snotty, wealthy mentality," says Denison. "I think she thought I was going to sell some inexpensive line of Avon or something like that. When I showed her the products, she said, 'Oh, these are way too expensive and this Nutriol smells too much like vitamins.' She just put the whole product line down."

But Denison didn't realize the depth of the woman's malice until she tried recruiting others in the woman's social circle. None of them would speak to Denison about the business. Her hostile prospect had gone out of her way to poison all her friends against Denison. The woman's cruelty might have paralyzed Denison, had she taken it personally. But Denison turned her attention resolutely to those markets that were still open to her.

"I just had to let it go," Denison recalls. "I had to sit down and tell myself not to be affected by that. I had to say 'That's okay, there's more people.'"

LEARNED HELPLESSNESS AND SELF-TALK

The importance of "self-talk"—the inner conversation you hold with yourself every day—in building self-esteem, has been written about for centuries by everyone from the gospel evangelists to motivational guru W. Clement Stone.

But the science of cognitive psychology has recently added support to this ancient wisdom. In 1966, psychologist Martin E. P. Seligman discovered that rats could be made to suffer depression. You simply have to subject them to repeated electric shocks. At first, they scramble to escape the shock chamber. But when they find no exit, they lay down on the metal shock plate and surrender to the pain. Once the rats have "learned helplessness," they will lie passively on the shock plate even after a door has been opened. The rats have learned that escape is impossible, so they don't even try to get away.

In the almost 30 years since that ground-breaking experiment, Seligman has revolutionized the thinking of psychology on self-esteem—and of the business world as well.

He discovered that people react much the same way as rats. They learn helplessness after suffering repeated reversals. And even when a way out is offered, they fail to take advantage of it.

Optimistic Self-Talk

The difference between normal rats and those who have been taught helplessness is their self-talk. The normal rats think, "I can escape from this pain by jumping or climbing out of this box." The helpless rats think, "No matter what I do, I cannot escape the pain, so I won't even try."

Through years of research, Seligman discovered that a person's degree of optimism or pessimism is entirely governed by the sort of self-talk he or she employs every day.

For example, suppose a prospect screams, "I hate you! I hate your products! Don't ever call me up again."

A person with a pessimistic style of self-talk will assume, "There must be something wrong with me. I must have done or said something in my presentation that offended this person."

A person with an optimistic style will assume that the other person is at fault. "That person must be having a really bad day!"

The three forms of damaging self-talk that Seligman identified are presented here. *Pervasiveness* is when you universalize one bad experience till it pervades your whole life. "What a day!" you might say after the offending phone call. "How can I stand eight hours more of this?" *Personalization* means blaming yourself. "I must have said something wrong." *Permanence* is imagining that your ill luck of the moment is a chronic condition of your life, as in, "This always happens to me! I never get good prospects."

Based upon his findings, Seligman devised a 20-minute test to identify people with an optimistic explanatory style. After instituting this test—the Seligman Attributional Style Questionnaire (SASQ)—in its screening procedure for new hirings in the late '80s, Metropolitan Life experienced a 50-percent increase in its share of the personal insurance market.

A Self-Esteem Program

The Wave-Three organization actually provides a structure, which, by its very nature, alters the explanatory style of ordinary people, turning them into Seligmanian superachievers.

"I really think that network marketing is a self-esteem program," says Denison. "You learn who you are and what you're willing to do, and how strong you really are. You start out, you work very hard, and you might feel like you're underpaid. But, at the end, you turn out to be a better person than you've ever been before. You blossom as a person through this business."

THE TAO OF SELLING

In the total sales culture, buying and selling will acquire new meaning. No longer the exclusive domain of merchants, moving product will become a metaphor of life itself—a development long foreshadowed in the annual "Everybody Sells" issue of *Success* magazine.

"I equate selling with living and breathing," wrote Scott DeGarmo, Editor and Publisher of *Sucess*. "Unless we are selling . . . then we are not truly alive."

In short, selling will become a spiritual act—a new path to self-actualization. In the pursuit of salesmanship, network marketers will develop mental and spiritual health—the very qualities they need to succeed at Wave-Three selling!

"In the last analysis, this is not just . . . about who earns the most," says DeGarmo, "for the greatest result of selling is the self-development of the individual. It shapes and toughens a person, exposing him or her to the constant stabs of rejection, the lonely battles of endurance, the self-discipline of constant preparation. . . . If you want to truly come to life, then prepare yourself to sell."

Set Goals

When Denison came out of her first marriage, her self-esteem was destroyed. But she fought her way back up through the power of visualization and goalsetting.

"I put up a big goal board of everything that I wanted to achieve," she says. "I pretended that I had 10 million dollars. And I cut out pictures from magazines of things that I wanted for my future, like cars and homes and clothes, and building a business all over the world, and having a happy family and being a great mom and a successful leader in Nu Skin."

"I was very focused, because I was so tired. I was really mad at not having what I wanted in my life."

The Payoff

Denison experienced the power of visualization in a remarkable way.

She and her new husband, Mark Rogow—a prosperous Nu Skin distributor she'd met at a convention—ended up playing a major role in opening the Japanese market for Nu Skin. One day, one of their distributors called and asked them to visit Japan, where he'd built a sizeable downline.

Denison and her husband wondered if the trip would be worth it. Japan had just been opened, and they imagined there could only be a handful of Nu Skin people there.

But the distributor said, "You don't understand, you have 54 qualifying executives in your downline!"

"Mark took out his calculator," says Denison, "and figured that out, and then he said, 'I think we're going to be there next week.'"

A Star Is Born . . .

Denison's first trip to Tokyo exceeded her wildest dreams. A chauffered Mercedes pulled up at the airport to whisk them to their hotel. Everything had been paid for. That night, the couple was taken to a first-class restaurant, where 250 people rose and applauded when Denison walked in the room.

"Everybody was all smiles and looking at us," she remembers.

Then the interpreter informed her, "You're going to tell your story tonight. This is your first meeting, and these are your people."

Denison could feel a hard lump of emotion in her throat as she mounted the podium and told her simple tale, through the interpreter. The audience of businesspeople, students, and top-level professionals hung spellbound on her every word.

"They loved it," she says, "because they don't see something like this happening often in their society, where a person who is cleaning houses becomes successful in business. Afterwards, there was a lot of bowing, of course, and a lot of 'Oh, your skin is so beautiful,' and 'Oh, that was a wonderful story.' "

In her speech, Denison spoke of the "board of goals" she had made, of the pictures she clipped from magazines, and of her dream of one day doing business all over the world.

"I told them that when I was a little girl, my favorite song was 'When You Wish Upon a Star,' " says Denison. "And after my speech, they looked me in the eye and said, 'We are part of your dream and your dream has just begun.' They're really mystical people in a sense. They believe in things. They believe in the dream."

Today, whenever Denison travels to Japan, she is treated like a movie star.

"I love Japan," she continues. "I'm looked up to as a hero there, because I have a success story."

A Dream Come True

All Denison's passion, faith, drive, and energy never succeeded in raising her above the status of a housemaid. But when she channeled those energies through a Wave-Three selling system, Denison won not only wealth but self-esteem.

"I've got a wonderful husband," she says. "I live in a 5,000-square-foot home, overlooking the bay of San Diego. I Rollerblade every day. I shop at the best stores. I travel all over the world. I spend time with my family and my daughter as much as I want. I have a life that few people could even imagine having . . . I feel really fortunate that I persevered and made it, and believed in my dreams and never gave up."

Chapter 6

WAVE-THREE PROSPECTING

E dgar Mitchell knew it was "sweaty palm time." That's astronaut jargon for a moment when survival hangs in the balance. The Apollo 14 lunar module had fired its engines at 60,000 feet and begun its descent to the moon. For the first 30,000 feet, all went well. Then it happened.

"You're not locked on," said the calm voice from mission control.

Their landing radar wasn't working. The astronauts were flying blind. A miscalculation could send their fragile spacecraft smashing into the rocky surface. The safe thing would have been to abort the mission. But the astronauts never considered that for a moment.

"We were very goal-oriented," Mitchell recalls. "After coming all that way, we would almost rather have crashed on the moon than busted the mission."

So they continued their descent.

Even the tiniest circuit in the lunar module had been tested and retested; procedures had been devised for each emergency; and backups existed for every system. No variable had been left to chance. But in the end, the mission hung upon the courage, training, and discipline of the crew.

Guided by the voice from the radio, the astronauts worked like madmen, toggling switches, punching in computer programs, their eyes sweeping the instrument panel in practiced scan patterns. They had only one minute in which to get the radar working. After that, they would be too close to the moon. They would have to turn back.

Mitchell remembers going into a state of detachment—almost as if he were separated from his body, viewing events from a great distance. No thought of danger or death entered his mind. Only the deep ecstasy of performing at his peak.

"I was totally focused on the task at hand," Mitchell recalls.

Barely seconds before the cut-off point, the radar suddenly switched on. They were minutes away from landing. Mitchell guided them in. Out the window, they saw the dust kicked up by their thrust, their spacecraft's lengthening shadow on the ground. The surface warning light told them their landing pads had touched down. They were on the moon.

"The main thing I felt," Mitchell recalls, "was a great sense of relief."

PROSPECTING—THE FIELD OF GLORY

Of course, at that moment, Mitchell must have felt quite a bit more than relief. Like Columbus on the shores of San Salvador, Mitchell and his fellow Apollo moonwalkers no doubt brooded on thoughts familiar only to a handful of history's greatest. Having been tested in history's most fearsome crucibles, they had proven themselves worthy.

Network marketers endure fearsome tests too, especially when it comes to canvassing and coldcalling. They don't gain much acclaim for their prospecting efforts. But they must bring to bear stores of courage and character not so different from those of great explorers and heroes.

Nowhere has the soothing impact of Wave Three been more vital—or more revolutionary—than in the area of

prospecting. Prospecting has always been the most ardu-
ous hurdle networkers face. Every day they confront a
world of hostile or indifferent strangers whose attention
they must capture and whose lives they must strive to
touch. How do you find new recruits? When you've found
them, how do you approach them? And once you've made
contact, how do you win them over?

Edgar Mitchell discovered that these are not easy
questions. In some ways, he found prospecting as challenging as landing on the moon! But as with his lunar landing,
Mitchell found the best approach was to detach himself
from his fears and *trust the system.*

"With the Apollo program, if we didn't have faith in the
system," says Mitchell, "and in ourselves and the team, we
shouldn't have been there. If you didn't have that, you
weren't ready for launch."

A Job for Heroes

Like so many networkers today, Edgar Mitchell was a
"white-collar refugee," pressed into the business through financial reverses. A scientist and philosopher rather than a
salesman, Mitchell found that his MIT doctorate ill-prepared
him for buttonholing strangers on the street.

"It was tough on my ego," Mitchell remembers. "I had
been in positions of considerable authority, responsibility
and skill. Now here I was in my '50s, approaching strangers
on the street. It was like going back and being a foot soldier
in the trenches."

Like most people, Mitchell has subsisted most of his
life on linear income—money paid in exchange for time.
His moon expedition, for example, earned him $81.

"The standard government per diem in those years
was nine dollars per day, if you had government meals and
quarters provided," Mitchell explains. "Well, our spacecraft
was government quarters, our meals were provided, and
we were gone nine days, so it equalled 81 bucks."

After retiring in 1972, Mitchell earned a lot more as a highly-paid lecturer and corporate consultant. But it was still linear income. That meant it could be cut off at any time. When a French shipyard he was consulting fell victim to a government-orchestrated takeover, Mitchell was given the ax.

"It cost me dearly," recalls Mitchell. "All the bonuses that I was supposed to receive I didn't receive. And I'd been gone from the U.S. for three years and lost all my contacts. I had to start my consulting practice all over again."

Mitchell knew it would take months or years to rebuild his contacts. He needed extra income. So Mitchell signed on as a distributor for Network 2000—an Independence, MO-based company selling U.S. Sprint long-distance service.

"I worked it just about full-time for two years," says Mitchell. "I used the three-foot rule. If anybody gets within three feet of you, you approach them, whether it's your waitress in a restaurant or the hotel staff when you check into a hotel. If you're sitting next to someone on an airplane, you try to turn the conversation around to your network marketing business."

Because he trusted the system and stuck with it, Mitchell succeeded in building a downline several hundred strong and achieving a monthly residual income as high as $1,700. He overcame his shyness by calling on the same inner strength that had landed him safely on the moon.

"I just said to myself, 'This needs to be done,' and then I went and did it," he says.

"LOW-IMPACT" PROSPECTING

Strength like Mitchell's will always stand networkers in good stead. But prospecting no longer demands quite so much heroism. Wave-Three networkers employ a "low-

impact" approach to prospecting that shields the distributor from many of the worst effects of his or her own fears,
flaws, and weaknesses. In the Wave-Three organization,
systems and technology amplify the prospecting power of
each networker. Choose the right company, with the right
tools, the right infrastructure, the right corporate image,
and the right prospecting system, and your downline will
grow, despite your deficiencies in sales expertise.

The Wave-Three System

Every upline leader has his or her own unique prospecting
system. You should always follow the system taught by
your upline. But no matter what minor differences in style
or approach your upline may practice, the fundamental
principles of prospecting will always be the same.

The Wave-Three system fuses those core insights and
prospecting principles that champion networkers have perfected through 50 years of experience. Many aspects of the
system are as old as salesmanship itself. Others are as up
to date as satellite conferences, voice broadcasts, and
three-way phone calls. But all have been proven in the
field. Together, they comprise a seamless mesh of standard-
ized procedures, which, when followed faithfully, will ensure success to any prospector.

In its broad strokes, the system can be distilled into
nine simple steps. They are presented here.

STEP #1: WRITE YOUR WARM LIST

Network marketers call it by many names. Warm market.
Center of influence. Comfort zone. But it all means the
same thing. It means those people closest to you. Friends,
relatives, co-workers. People whom you know by their first

names. That's your primary market. Target them before you target anyone else.

"According to social psychologists," says Mark Yarnell, "anyone over the age of 25 knows 2,000 people on a first-name basis. But you need a triggering device to help you recall them."

That device is your *warm list*. Sit down and start listing all the people you personally know. Don't worry about where they live. As long as your company offers distributorships in their state, you can recruit them and sponsor them long-distance. It may take a few days before your memory yields every name. And you may never reach your target of 2,000. Yarnell, in his first stab, only came up with 1,700 names. But, if you shoot for the stars, you may just reach the moon.

In his book, *Being the Best You Can Be in MLM,* noted trainer John Kalench recommends these additional exercises to help stir your memory:

- Copy out every name from your address book, including from old address books, if you save them.
- In your mind, review the different areas of your life—family, church, work, hobbies. List every person you can think of associated with each area.
- Hold brainstorming sessions with groups of friends and family to try to recall people you've forgotten.

"You make your list of everybody you've ever known in your life, without qualification," says Yarnell. "You don't think, 'Well, he's a lawyer, he won't do it,' or 'She's a maid or housewife, she can't do it.' You put down everybody. Your first four to five months in this business should be dedicated exclusively to contacting your warm market."

Some networkers advise against targeting friends and family. They say this could alienate you from the people you care about the most. But Yarnell counsels a more assertive approach.

"The only person who doesn't go after their friends or family," says Yarnell, "either doesn't believe that their friends and family respect them or doesn't believe in our industry in the first place. If you knew for sure you could get people to earn $30,000 a month, wouldn't you want to get your own family there quickest?"

STEP #2: TARGET 30 PEOPLE A DAY

Action is essential in building momentum for your downline. Mark Yarnell challenges distributors to target 30 people a day, five days a week. If you sustain this pace for one year, says Yarnell, the odds are great that you'll build a lucrative money machine.

Of the 600 people you target each month, about 570 will turn you down, says Yarnell. Maybe 5 percent, or 30 people per month, will join your downline. Of those 30, only one may become a leader—that is, a fulltime distributor in your downline. The other 29 will drop out or become wholesale buyers.

With all that attrition, why does the system work? Because of the laws of probability. You're bound to come up with at least one leader a month, Yarnell explains. And that's all you need. By the end of one year, you'll have 12 frontline distributors, all moving at least $5,000 worth of product per month. Yarnell says the odds are that 3 of them will be moving at least $50,000 per month at that point.

STEP #3: SELL FROM THE HEART

Many readers will be daunted by the challenge of targeting 30 people a day. Where do you meet all these people? What do you say to them? How do you break the ice? How do you hook them?

The traditional salesperson responds with an arsenal of prepackaged icebreakers, sales pitches, stock answers to objections, and closing techniques. Even a novice can be helped by such tools. At the very least, a prepackaged sales script may help you feel more secure. The best source of such scripts is your own upline. You might also consult Dennis Windsor's excellent manual, *The Script Book,* available through the *Upline Resources* catalog at (800) 800-6349.

However, sales scripts are really a high-impact technique. They are most effective in helping sales professionals pitch huge numbers of people on products that the salesperson personally cares little or nothing about. High-impact selling relies upon brute force. To do it well, you must expend huge amounts of energy and have an unusually gregarious personality. And usually, the prospect will sense your coldness and detachment from the product.

"I am anti-script," says John Fogg, editor of *Upline.* "If I read you a script, you're going to hear it as a script. It's a turnoff."

The Wave-Three approach comes from the heart. It is an outgrowth of your natural enthusiasm for the product. Through retailing your product, you find the recruits you're looking for.

"If you're selling weight loss products," says Sandy Elsberg, a distributor for Life Extension International, "you can get one good customer each week just because you went down four dress sizes or four notches on your belt. Your friends and family, neighbors and co-workers will notice changes in spirit, smiles, a slimmer you, a new car. They will actually come to you and ask you what is going on, why you look and act so differently. What if you get one good customer a week this way, times 50 weeks a year? What if five of those 50 turn out to be as successful as you with the products and choose to become distributors?"

Sincere enthusiasm can win over strangers just as easily.

"Let people overhear you in public places," suggests Elsberg. "I sell product in restaurants to the people in the booth behind me who overhear my conversations. I sell products in clothing stores to people in the booth next door trying on clothes. I swear to you, if your enthusiasm is high, you can get people to follow you off elevators."

If you truly love and use the product, the right "sales script" will come to you unconsciously, in the same way that you manage to find the right words to recommend a good movie, a restaurant, or a beautician to your friends. And your pitch will be all the more effective because it's delivered in your own words, in your own style, and it comes from your heart. The key to Wave-Three selling is simply to find a product that really excites you.

You Have to Be Sold Before You Can Sell

Kirby and Cynthia Wright found out the hard way that you have to be sold before you can sell. If you're passionate about the product, prospecting has a strange way of taking care of itself. But if you're not, all the technique in the world won't win you a single recruit.

All Cynthia wanted out of life was one thing—to escape the nine-to-five grind. She worked 12-hour days as branch manager for a temporary help office, and hardly ever saw her three-year-old daughter. "I would get very frustrated at my husband," she admits. "I would say to him, 'When are you going to be rich enough so I can quit my job?'"

Her husband Kirby set out manfully to find the answer through network marketing. First, he dragged Cynthia to a training session for a company that sold water filters.

"They were talking about how to install these water filters," remembers Kirby, "what type of washer you used, the various bolts and wrenches you needed, and how you laid the towel down under the thing so you wouldn't get water on your back. It was like being a plumber. Cindy and I just kind of looked at each other, and I knew this wasn't going to work."

That Shifty Look . . .

Nevertheless, Kirby gave it a shot. That was a big mistake. He tried to push the filters on his friends and neighbors, even though he didn't really want one himself. "As soon as I started talking about water filters," he says, "people would kind of roll their eyes at me and say, 'I gotta go.' "

Deep in his heart, Kirby just didn't like what he was selling. And people sensed it. "I felt it was overpriced," he admits. "I couldn't sponsor anybody because I didn't believe in it myself." In the end, Kirby sold one filter, and stored the rest in his garage—$5,000 worth.

Next, the couple signed on with a cosmetics company. "It just wasn't for me," admits Kirby sheepishly. A skincare company came next. But the detailed, biochemical dissertation with which their sponsor explained each product intimidated Cynthia.

"It was too complicated," she says. "I knew I couldn't do it."

The Wrights dabbled with MLM for more than three years.

"In all that time," says Kirby, "I sponsored one person total, sold maybe five hundred dollars worth of product, and spent $11,000. I felt like a bigtime loser. And my wife was beginning to think I was a loser, too."

The Winning Difference

Like clockwork, the Wrights would fight every month when the bills came due. Cynthia blamed their plight on MLM. They were wasting money on these crazy schemes, she said. Kirby was discouraged, too. But something inside just wouldn't let him quit.

"I was convinced that there was something out there for me," he says. "There just had to be."

Kirby was right. He soon discovered a new company called Reliv, which sold a nutritional drink. Cynthia seethed when she heard he'd signed up for yet another MLM scam. When would he ever learn?

For a week, Cynthia evaded Kirby's attempts to make her try the Reliv drink. Each day, she waited until Kirby left the room, then poured it down the sink. Finally, to humor him, Cynthia agreed to sample it. After just one week, she felt like a new woman.

"I was staying up later. Before, I used to fall asleep as soon as I got my daughter into bed. Now I was up till midnight. I noticed that my cravings for junk food were going away. French fries and hamburgers were less and less appealing."

"I got excited at that point, because I thought this is something that I could put my Mom and Dad on, my family and neighbors. It was something that I could talk to them about."

And talk she did. Five months later, Cynthia went full-time in the business. Kirby followed her in another three months. By the eleventh month, they had attained Reliv's top achievement level, raking in $8,000 a month. Today, their yearly income is about $250,000 a year. The couple who could barely sponsor a single person had been magically transformed into champion prospectors—all because they'd found a product they could believe in.

STEP #4: FOLLOW-UP

When you make contact with a new prospect, it's important to follow up by phone within 24 hours. To keep things moving, network marketing trainer David Roller recommends calling your new prospects before calling your distributors. When you sit down at the phone for your daily calling time, the natural temptation is to make the easy calls first—in most cases, those people you've already signed up and already know. Often, these easy calls linger on so long that you never get to your prospects!

"By following this system," says Roller in his book, *How to Make Big Money in Multi-Level Marketing,* "you will end up making all your phone calls, including the most important ones—those to your prospects."

STEP #5: USE THE QUICK QUALIFIER

You can begin to sort or qualify your prospects the moment you make your first pitch. In his book *Big Al Tells All,* champion trainer Tom "Big Al" Schreiter recommends that you ask each prospect the two "magic questions." They are: (1) Do you want to earn some extra money? and (2) Are you willing to set aside 6 to 10 hours per week?

According to Big Al, these are the only two qualities that matter in a prospect. Network marketing is the great leveler. In this arena, janitors often outperform presidents of companies. And a prospect who has no interest today, may be hot to trot in six months. The only real issue is to find out whether they have the time and desire right now.

If your prospect answers no to the two magic questions, you probably don't need to waste any more time with him or her.

STEP #6: THE VIDEO DROP

In years past, network marketers harangued prospects for hours with arguments about the company, the industry, the compensation plan. The point was to persuade an interested prospect on the spot, even if it meant riding him till long after midnight.

But in Wave-Three prospecting, that's the last thing you want to do. Avoid prolonged discussions like the plague. Your goal is far easier and far more modest. Just get your prospect to watch a video!

This technique is called the *video drop*.

"Since you've expressed an interest in this business opportunity," you might say, "I'd like you to promise me two things. I'm going to send you a video, by Fed-Ex. You'll get it tomorrow morning. It's only 15 minutes long. Promise me that, one, you'll watch the video. And promise me, two, that when I call you the day after tomorrow, you'll tell me what you thought of it."

And that's it. The conversation takes one minute. It doesn't require you to stick your neck out or put your ego on the line. And if you have fifty videos, you can have fifty such conversations a day—and prospect that many people.

Two days later, you ask your prospect what was interesting about the video. His or her answer will tell you a lot.

Audiotapes Are Easier

Often, people are too busy for your video. It may only be 15 minutes long, but your prospect still has to walk over to the VCR, pop in the cassette, turn on the TV, and spend 15 minutes giving that video full attention.

Yarnell recommends offering your prospect a choice of video or audiotape. Or maybe both at once! The same prospect who doesn't feel like watching your video at the end of a long day may just decide to pop your audiotape into his dashboard tape deck while sitting in a traffic jam the next morning.

Screening by Video

The video acts as a second-line "screening" or "qualifying" filter. It weeds out good prospects from bad.

When you ask your prospect how he or she liked the video, be prepared for anything. They might just throw it back at you with some nasty comment. But so what?

"You've saved yourself a great deal of time and effort, haven't you?" says John Fogg, editor of *Upline*. "Just say 'Send me back the video . . .' and you've only wasted a few minutes of your time."

STEP #7: LISTEN

But what if your prospect seems interested? A great deal hangs upon your reaction to your prospect's reaction. In Wave-Three prospecting, you're not expected to haggle with your prospect or counter every objection. At this point, all you need to do is move on to Step 8 in the prospecting process.

Ask your prospect, "What did you like best about the video?" And then listen closely to the answer.

"I've learned that the questions that really work are aimed at what's the best, what's the most interesting, what's the most important?" says Fogg. "Because that gets you talking in a positive way. That taps into your imagination and your creativity, rather than questions about what's wrong, what's the problem? Those tend to be down questions."

As your prospect answers, you must listen for any hint about what it is he or she really wants from this opportunity.

"Once they take a look at the business," says Fogg, "they begin to reveal what's really important to them in their lives, what their values are, what problems they have that they need to solve."

Maybe your prospect is most concerned with making some extra income to get out of debt. Maybe he's looking for a part-time job for his wife. Maybe she wants to earn enough to retire in three years. Virtually anything your prospect says, at this point, provides a cue for you to suggest that the two of you move on to Step 8.

Howard Solomon of Quorum suggests a slightly different approach:

"Ask them what they dislike the most about what they're doing," he says, "and if they had to make a wish list, what would be the number one item on their wish list that their present situation would never allow them to achieve."

Here, too, virtually any answer the prospect gives opens a door to pitch your opportunity as the solution.

STEP #8: MEETING OR TELECONFERENCE

A well-equipped Wave-Three organization will actually offer four different options, at this point, for moving your prospect closer to a decision. You can invite him to a live meeting, bring her to a satellite conference in someone's home, hook up your prospect to your company's next teleconference, or proceed to Step 9—setting up a three-way meeting with your upline sponsor.

All four methods are extremely low-impact. If you bring your prospect to a live home or hotel meeting, your upline will do the presentation for you, and the synergy of all those enthusiastic people gathered together in one room will do most of your persuading for you.

A satellite or teleconference requires virtually no effort at all on your part. Simply get your prospect to show up at the right place and time or place a call at the right time. The top presenters in your company will do the rest for you.

But maybe your prospect doesn't feel like waiting until the next meeting or teleconference. Maybe your prospect is ready *now* to meet with your upline sponsor. If so, you can always skip Step 8, and come back to it later. Meetings and teleconferences are just as valuable for enthusiastic new trainees as they are for undecided prospects.

Proceed to Step 9!

STEP #9: THE TWO-ON-ONE CLOSE

"Videos don't sign people up," says John Fogg. "People sign people up."

As soon as you get a positive reaction to your video, you must get that prospect in front of a live human being as quickly as possible to close the deal. This is the *low-impact close*. In a three-way phone presentation, one recruiter talks and the other just observes. You're the observer. All you need to do is get your prospect to commit to a three-way phone call, with you and your sponsor. You just stay on the line, listen, and learn.

There are a lot of reasons why a team of two works better than one. For one thing, there's power in numbers. You have more confidence when you work with a partner. If you're prospecting a friend or family member, they're less likely to waste time on small talk if there's a stranger on the other line. Also, your prospect will tend to think more of your opportunity simply because it's already convinced two people, rather than one.

When you ask your prospect to meet with your sponsor, whether by phone or in person, it's important to remember that he or she doesn't know what to expect and may be a little anxious. Make sure you let your prospect know that the meeting entails no obligation. That takes the pressure off.

STEP #10: GET A COMMITMENT

Congratulations. You've closed a sale. You've signed up a new recruit. But there's one final step to the screening process. Until your recruit makes a commitment to actually work the business, he or she is nothing but a name on a list.

A new recruit shows commitment by filling out a product order. Many new prospectors are too timid to press for this. They're so excited to have signed up a new recruit that they don't want to "scare him away" by insisting that he actually start working the business.

MLM trainer David Roller advises prospectors to observe the "You-Can't-Lose-What-You-Don't-Have" Principle. In fact, you don't really have a new recruit until he or she has committed to the business. Let's say the worst happens. You ask your new recruit to buy $500 worth of inventory and set up five three-way phone appointments with people on his warm-list. Your prospect cries, "No! I don't have time for all that. I guess I don't really want to be in this business."

Have you really lost anything? No. Because this recruit never really wanted to work the business in the first place. You haven't lost a thing, because you never had anything to lose.

Avoid "Info" Overload

One of the most common mistakes is to provide your prospect with too much information. Most prospects don't want a detailed lecture on the strengths of your company. They just want to know whether it will survive. They don't need a doctoral dissertation on your product. They just want to know if people will buy it. And, in most cases, they're not much concerned about how the compensation plan works. They just want to know how much money they can make.

Avoid the temptation to load your prospect down with every video, brochure, and training manual that your company provides. That's the best way to ensure that your prospect will look at none of them.

Use one good prospecting video, preferably no longer than 15 minutes. The rest of the information can wait till he or she is in training.

On Your Own

You won't be able to rely on your sponsor forever. After three months or so, you should be able to make your own presentations, and to act as the "talker" on your three-way calls. Now you have to teach your own recruits how to do it!

You need to become a master of the Wave-Three persuasion system. (See Chapter 7 for details.)

LEVERAGED PROSPECTING THROUGH ADVERTISING

Many networkers attempt to leverage their prospecting efforts through such means as advertising and direct mail. Experienced networkers advise beginners to steer clear of such distractions. To use them properly, you usually have to spend a lot of money. They can also become psychological crutches for distributors who fear face-to-face selling. The flurry of activity surrounding placing an ad or sending out a mailing makes distributors feel that they are doing something. But they'd probably get a lot better results just by picking up the phone and hitting the warm list.

Nevertheless, networkers at all levels should be aware that these techniques exist. And advancing technology is bringing the day ever closer when leveraged prospecting techniques will come within the reach even of the average network marketer.

ADVERTISING IS A LONG-TERM COMMITMENT

Print is the favorite medium of network-marketing advertisers. Opportunity ads can be found in daily and weekly newspapers, magazines, and free shoppers' papers. Radio and television are used less often, although the spread of cable TV has encouraged more and more companies to use direct-response infomercials.

Most experienced networkers agree that one-time ads are a waste of time. To achieve real results, you need to advertise regularly over a long period. That allows you to take advantage of special bulk rates from the publication where you place your ad, thus making your ad cost-effective, no matter how sparse the response. It also builds credibility for your advertisement, in the mind of the prospect. Many potential prospects will not respond to your ad the first two or three times they see it. But, after several times, they'll start to think of it as an established "institution" and will tend to be both more curious and more trusting.

Your Perfect Ad Copy

What should your ad say?

Life Extension International distributor Jerry Rubin says, "Write the ad that would have gotten you. Try to think of one sentence that you would answer. That's your ad."

There are no hard and fast rules for writing ad copy, except that you should avoid any hint of false advertising. It's not only unethical, it fails to pull the sort of prospects you want.

Let's say you ran an ad like this one, taken from *Big Al's How to Create a Recruiting Explosion:*

"HELP WANTED
Earn $300-500 a month part-time. Free training.
Unlimited potential for leaders.
Call 999-9999."

According to Big Al, the problem with this ad is that it seems to promise a salaried job. And if you promise people a job, they'll expect you to deliver one. Prospects answering these ads may feel tricked when they're offered instead a chance to invest their own time and money in a business venture. Big Al suggests this alternative:

"BUSINESS OPPORTUNITY
Own your own part-time business. Major network marketing company looking for part-time distributors. Less than $100 to get started.
Call 999-9999."

Direct Mail Is for Experts Only

The first rule of prospecting by mail is . . . don't do it!

As Big Al points out, sending out mailings is expensive, time-wasting, and unproductive. You can pay a list broker up to $50 per thousand names for a good list. Add in the cost of company flyers to send in your mailing, postage stamps, envelopes, postage-paid return envelopes, and a mailing of only 50,000 names could cost you well over $20,000.

Moreover, there's no guarantee that you'll really get the two-percent return from your mailing that direct-mail professionals predict.

"There is no average return percentage in mail order," says Big Al, "because there is no average mail order."

Direct mail is for experts. They have the money, the list consultants, the top-end copywriters, and graphic designers to pull it off. And if they drop $20,000 on a mailing that doesn't pull, they're still in business.

Until you hit the big time, you'd better stick to two-on-one meetings.

The "Techno" Edge

Lest I seem overly discouraging, I will acknowledge that leveraged prospecting has a future in network marketing.

The key will be new technology. As computers get cheaper and more user-friendly, direct mail and other leveraged forms of prospecting will become increasingly accessible to average distributors.

In the near future, more and more distributors will prospect by means of direct-response ads equipped with toll-free voice-mail numbers. Respondents will receive personalized "merge" letters, produced by PC. Direct mailings will also feature voice-mail numbers, which have already proven effective in vastly increasing response rates.

But these technologies lie mainly in the hands of PC buffs today. It still costs several thousand dollars to equip yourself with the requisite hardware and software, and it still takes a lot of your precious time away from cold-calling. For the time being, the average distributor should stick with the phone and a warm market.

Find Your Pearl

The "oyster" story has been making the rounds of the network-marketing industry for years, in different versions. I don't know who invented it originally. But it encapsulates perfectly the proper methodology for screening your prospects.

Once upon a time, there were two pearl divers, Stavros and Giorgos, who lived on a Greek island. Stavros was a big success, but Giorgos could barely feed his family. One day, Stavros offered to dive with Giorgos, to see if he could help his less fortunate colleague.

Giorgos dove to the bottom of the sea and picked out a good-looking oyster. Then he brought it up to the surface, carried it lovingly to the beach, and proceeded to cut the oyster open with his knife.

"Why did you come up so soon?" asked Stavros. "You wasted a whole dive to get just one oyster!"

"I know what I'm doing," says Giorgos. "I have a feeling about this oyster. There's just something about it."

Stavros watched in silence as his friend finished prying the oyster apart. Alas, there was no pearl! Giorgos carefully closed the oyster, cupped it between his hands and sat motionless, rocking back and forth with his eyes closed.

"Giorgos, what are you doing now?" asked Stavros.

"I believe in this oyster," said Giorgos. "If I nurse it and keep it warm, maybe it will grow a pearl eventually, out of gratitude."

Shaking his head, Stavros walked away. It was getting late in the day, and he needed to get some work done. While Giorgos nursed his special oyster, Stavros made a solo dive, scooping up 100 oysters into his bucket, bringing them back to the beach, and methodically cutting open every one. Any oyster that didn't have a pearl, Stavros threw back in the water.

At dusk, Stavros checked on his friend. Giorgos was still nursing his empty oyster.

"Any luck?" asked Giorgos.

"Why, yes," Stavros replied. "I threw away 95 empty oysters. But I found five with pearls in them. I think I'll take my wife out to the *taverna* tonight to celebrate."

"Stavros, you always were a lucky slob," said Giorgos.

It's Not Luck

Of course, luck has nothing to do with it. The champion prospector is always the one who sorts through 100 bad prospects . . . to come up with five pearls!

Many networkers behave just like Giorgos. They keep returning to the same prospect again and again, even though he or she keeps saying no. Of course, the Giorgos's don't like being rejected. But it's a lot easier to endure one rejection from a prospect they know, than to risk a hundred rejections from a horde of perfect strangers. They justify their inactivity by telling themselves they're working on the stubborn prospect.

Don't waste your time pleading or arguing with people who seem closed or unduly skeptical. If you have to coax them to join, you'll probably just have to coax them to work every day, after they're signed up. Follow the principle of the "oyster" story—throw empty ones back in the water.

"It's a matter of sorting through enough people," says Quorum distributor Howard Solomon. "Look for the ones that want to do it."

What to do with empty oysters? Of course, in network marketing, no oyster is completely empty. It may not contain the pearl of a potential frontline leader. But even the most dismal prospect could still be turned into a wholesale buyer. He or she can also provide referrals to other prospects, who might themselves turn out to be pearl-bearers.

It never hurts to ask!

YOUR TARGET MARKET

The 80/20 rule states that 80 percent of your business will be done by 20 percent of your downline distributors. So you've got to make sure you get the right distributors.

The best way to meet small business owners and other motivated professionals is through community organizations. Sign up for courses and events at your local Chamber of Commerce. John Fogg of *Upline* recommends approaching local groups like the Lions, Rotary, and Kiwanis and volunteering to speak on a subject like "Network Marketing—Wave of the Future or Illegal Pyramid Scam?"

Small Business Owners

Small business owners provide an excellent fishing ground for MLM prospecting. For one thing, they already understand the difficulties of running a business. They've already wrestled with the big life decisions involved in deciding to go it alone. They are also more likely to have the kind of credit and cash reserves they'll need to become a frontline leader.

Another reason small business owners are ripe for network marketing is that they're *hurting.*

"You've got to go for people who are feeling pain right now," says Tom Hill of Nu Skin. "And that's your small business owners."

As Hill points out, small business owners today are reeling from the rising costs of taxes, worker benefits, and government regulations. Many are wide open to hear about a way of doing business that sidesteps the bureaucracy.

"Terry and I have 5,000 distributors in our downline," says Hill, "but we don't have to pay them a dime of social security, health care benefits, unemployment, nothing. And, if one of them slips and falls, I don't get a workers' comp filing. So you get the benefits of a traditional business without the headaches. When you explain that to a lot of small business owners, they're very open to the idea."

Recruit Other Networkers

Some networkers advocate seeking your leaders exclusively from the ranks of experienced network marketers.

"It's like a professional sports team when they start up a new franchise," says Quorum's Howard Solomon. "Who do they staff the team with? They don't write an ad in the newspaper, do they? They go after other professional sports teams. They recruit and trade and draft professional players. That's one way of doing network marketing."

Solomon recommends that even beginning prospectors ask around among their friends to see who they know in network marketing.

"Find people who are dissatisfied with their present company," says Solomon, "people who are looking for a better vehicle."

Go Global

The Wave-Three revolution has opened a fertile prospecting field utterly unknown to networkers in the past—foreign markets.

Tom and Terry Hill have downlines in Hong Kong, Australia, New Zealand, Japan, and other countries. On their own, they never could have handled the complexities of building an overseas empire. But Nu Skin's global infrastructure made it almost easy. Indeed, most of the time, the Hills don't even have to leave home to recruit in those countries!

"One of my strongest distributors is a lady in Sydney, Australia, whom I've never met," says Tom Hill. "I do a lot of phone work with her. We fax and mail information back and forth. And I send her audio and videotapes for training."

Whenever necessary, the Hills communicate with their foreign downlines via global teleconference arranged by the parent company.

Nu Skin's infrastructure handles all the forbidding technical details of overseas business, which keep most average people confined within their own borders. Taxes, fees, customs, export-import licenses—all that is set up by the company in advance before they open a country to Nu Skin distributors. Company computers also insulate distributors from the maddening intricacies of currency conversion.

"Every month we get a printout," says Hill. "It goes country by country, giving all the volume we've moved there, with a breakdown in U. S. dollars of what we earned."

USE THE CORPORATE IMAGE

It's a lot easier to get a prospect's attention when you represent a multimillion dollar company with an established track record. Wave-Three distributors have learned to leverage corporate image as a powerful recruiting tool.

Tom Hill used it to particular advantage in his overseas ventures. He checked into the Hong Kong Hilton with a list of some 300 leads, many of them referrals from his downline, and others drawn from a library reference book listing Hong Kong business owners.

"I targeted company presidents with sales of $10–$50 million a year," says Hill.

As a former stockbroker for Merrill-Lynch, Hill had made plenty of cold-calls to company owners and CEOs. He knew how hard it was to get them on the phone. Top-level executives in America lived behind fortress walls, ever on their guard against unsolicited sales pitches. But Hill found prospecting a lot easier overseas.

Hill recruited one Hong Kong real-estate developer who'd made a fortune from building projects in Vietnam and elsewhere in the Far East. The man was tired of having to raise millions in capital every time he launched a new venture. He was looking for deals with a low cost of entry.

"I called him and introduced myself as a businessman from the U.S. representing a multimillion-dollar corporation," says Hill. "I told him I'd like the chance to meet with him and discuss some opportunities. He booked an appointment."

Hill met the man in the lobby of his hotel. After making his 20-minute presentation, Hill sat back and sucked in his breath, preparing for the worst. An American executive might have felt hoodwinked. He might have lost his temper, furious at having wasted his time on a network-marketing pitch. But, to his relief, Hill found that Asian businessmen have a more enlightened attitude.

"He signed up on the spot," says Hill. "He said, 'Let's get it going.'"

The last Hill heard, the man was doing exceptionally well. That's not surprising, considering the extraordinary work ethic Hill observed among Asian businessmen.

"Those guys go 24 hours," he marvels. "And talk about high tech! We'd go out to dinner and they'd all have their portable phones and portable fax machines. They love to fax and talk on those portable phones. It's almost constant."

Without Nu Skin's deep overseas infrastructure, Hill would never have gained access to that remarkable work ethic. Nor would he have enjoyed the sheer adventure of wheeling and dealing among the high rollers of the Pacific Rim.

Unlimited Potential

Nothing will ever take the dread out of cold-calling, nor the sting from rejection. But the low-impact approach of Wave-Three prospecting gives you a power unknown to salespeople of yesteryear. It gives you the power to focus every iota of your time, effort, and ingenuity on a single purpose, without distraction. That purpose is meeting people and persuading them to enlist in your opportunity.

"Put all your eggs in one basket," said Andrew Carnegie, "then watch that basket."

Carnegie understood that the force of an individual's concentrated effort is such that no obstacle can withstand it. So it is with the Wave-Three prospector, whose only job is to dream, plan, and work the system. If one but follows the procedures, the loftiest goals are sure to be realized.

Chapter 7

WAVE-THREE PERSUASION

Imagine that you've just persuaded a skeptical prospect to take a look at your opportunity. He watches your 15-minute video, and wants to know more. He speaks to your upline sponsor on a three-way call, but still isn't sure. You invite him to a live opportunity meeting, but he's busy and doesn't like crowds.

What do you do next?

In the past, the answer was . . . nothing. Nothing except pile on more brochures and photocopied fact sheets that he'll never read. Nothing except hammer at him by phone and in person until he finally tells you to drop dead. Or back off and maintain a friendship with him over many weeks and months, waiting passively for the right time to start pitching him again.

Today, however, there are other options.

THE WAVE-THREE PERSUASION SYSTEM

Wave-Three networkers have perfected a wealth of new methods that enable you to amplify your persuasive power during critical moments of the selling process. Among them are flashy new technologies such as satellite meetings and teleconferences. More subtle but just as powerful is the more traditional array of fine-tuned systems for handling objections, breaking down prejudices, and working with your downline to draw in prospects through meetings and home parties.

But all these techniques are bound together by a single principle—they enable you to leverage the knowledge, efforts, and training of others to do your selling for you. The key, as always, is to trust the system, and don't try to reinvent the wheel.

Electronic Intervention

Perhaps the purest example of Wave-Three persuasion is the company teleconference. It requires no effort on your part whatsoever. But it's remarkably effective in moving your toughest prospects along toward a decision.

For example, in the situation described above, you would simply ask your stubborn prospect to dial a certain number at a specific time and listen in. Your company will do the rest.

"Just listen for 25 minutes," you tell him. "If you don't find it interesting, hang up, and there's no further obligation."

It's an incredibly low-pressure sale. Your prospect calls the number and hears a professional announcer greeting the "attendees," and announcing how many people are listening in on the call—a number that could range from several hundred to thousands. The audience may even be international, with people listening in from many different countries. The sheer scope of the audience will impress your prospect.

Then the show begins. The announcer introduces and interviews a number of company luminaries, who might be anyone from the founder and president, to the top trainer or a successful new distributor with a rags-to-riches story. With all the glitz and glamor of a Hollywood talk show, the teleconference sells the product, the company, and the network-marketing industry itself. After 25 minutes, your prospect may not be thoroughly sold on your opportunity. But he now knows it's something big.

The Speakerphone Meeting

When Kirby and Cynthia Wright held their first meeting for Reliv, they had been with the Chesterfield, MO-based company for only two weeks.

"We knew nothing," admits Cynthia. "We had five prospects sitting in our livingroom, and we had no idea what to say to them."

But the Wrights didn't have to say anything. They were holding a *speakerphone meeting*. At the appointed time, they phoned their sponsor, Tom Pinnock, who lived hundreds of miles away in Orlando. Their sponsor delivered, through the speakerphone, a 30-minute sales pitch to a rapt audience. Three of the five prospects signed up on the spot.

"We did this at every meeting for the first 30 days," recalls Cynthia.

The Wrights discovered that speakerphone meetings generated a mystique about their sponsor that helped their sales efforts.

"It actually creates a little mystery about it," says Kirby. "Because they can't see him, they get intrigued."

When Pinnock finally drove up to personally conduct a meeting in the Wrights' livingroom, he had become a micro-celebrity.

"Everybody was dying to meet him," says Cynthia. "We had 30 people at our house the night he came."

Use OPS (Other People's Sizzle)

Old-time MLMers had to be masters of sales sizzle. But Wave-Three distributors use OPS—Other People's Sizzle. Any distributor with $500 and 20 minutes to spare can buy and install a satellite dish that will transform his home into a mini-convention center. Your prospects can watch a company presentation right in your living room featuring all the hoopla of a political convention over beers and pizza—and you don't need an ounce of training or sales skill to present it!

"We did a 30-minute broadcast from a huge regional conference in Dallas," says Reliv's Kirby Wright. "Thousands of prospects watched it all over the country, in living rooms, in hotel conference rooms, wherever. They got to hear the president of the company, the inventor of the product, a lot of the successful distributors. It was extremely well-received."

Satellite and telephone conferences inject professional sizzle right into your selling process, letting your prospect know that there are thousands more people out there participating in your opportunity. The presentation is polished. The talent is top-notch. You rely completely on the packaged slickness of others. And after it's over, you're free to devote your energies to the fun part of the selling process—relating to your prospect as a friend.

The Commando Factor

Nowadays, we make war with smart bombs and computerized, Tomahawk missiles. But Special Forces commandos still practice the primitive arts of hand-to-hand combat. Indeed, their training in the use of fists, feet, and knives is far more intense and systematic than ever before. That's because today's warrior must be as dangerous to the enemy naked and unarmed as he is when fitted with the latest night-vision goggles and shoulder-launched Stinger missiles.

Just so, Wave-Three sales commandos must drill themselves in the doctrine of "hand-to-hand salesmanship." All the technology in the world will not help you, if, when the TV falls dead, the video ends, and the teleconference signs off, you find yourself staring like an idiot at your prospect, groping for the right words.

Hand-to-Hand Selling

Hand-to-hand selling is still the only truly interactive phase of the persuasion process. It's only when talking to another human being that your prospects will have the chance to voice their objections and have their deepest questions answered.

In the beginning stages of your business, your upline sponsor will take care of this for you, through three-way meetings or phone calls. But eventually, your sponsor is going to kick you out of the nest. You'll have to make your own presentation and teach others how to do it.

The best method, to begin with, is always the method taught by your upline. But as you master those fundamentals, you will want to expand your repertoire with an arsenal of tried-and-true persuasive tools.

A SIX-STEP APPROACH

Wave-Three persuasion is a low-pressure selling process. Its purpose is not to close a sale, but to offer choices and possibilities. Your goal is to persuade your prospects that your way of living and doing business is a lot easier, more fun, and more lucrative than theirs. Below is a Six-Step approach to persuasion, synthesizing the best thinking to date of leading MLM trainers and upline leaders.

STEP #1: BUILD RAPPORT

You don't have to take a Dale Carnegie course to build rapport with people. All you have to do is show a sincere interest in them. Leading MLM trainer John Kalench recommends the "How-are-you?" technique. When you meet with your prospect, ask "How are you?" They'll probably brush you off with a half-hearted "Fine, thank you." That's when you lean forward and ask, "No, really. How are you?"

Listen very closely and patiently to what your prospect says next. It could be anything. And it really doesn't matter what they say. Just keep your prospect talking, as long as you can. When they falter, urge them on with phrases like, "Tell me more about that." By the time your prospects are talked out, they'll have the uncanny feeling that they have found a rare kindred spirit. And it will only take a few minutes.

STEP #2: EMPLOY THE ABC TECHNIQUE

"Would you ever try to pour hot coffee into a thermos with the lid still on?" asks Leonard Clements, publisher of *MarketWave*. "Could you put a video cassette into your VCR if it already had a cartridge in it? Of course not. Unfortunately, the way that most people prospect for MLM partners makes about as much sense."

According to Clements, most MLM prospectors try to force network marketing down people's throats, without adequately preparing them. To solve this problem, Clements has developed what he calls "The ABC Technique."

Clements cites a market research company that once performed a survey of nonbusiness owners, asking them "Have you ever considered owning your own business?"

Just about 85 percent answered yes to that, says Clements. The next question asked was, "Why didn't you ever go ahead and do it?" In almost every case, the respondents gave the same four reasons:

- It takes too much money.
- It takes too much time.
- It's too much of a risk.
- I don't know how to do it.

"The beauty of network marketing is that it blows all four of those objections right out of the water," says Clements. "It completely obliterates them."

To illustrate this, Clements suggests asking your prospect whether he or she would undertake a business that:

- Has total startup costs under $500 and income potential higher than the earnings of some Fortune 500 CEOs. ("It doesn't take too much money.")
- Requires total time investment as little as 10–20 hours a week. ("It doesn't take too much time.")
- Allows them to continue working at their present job until the income from their business is sufficient to earn them at least an equal income. ("It doesn't require too much risk.")
- Comes complete with another company that will take care of all research and development, payroll, shipping, taxes, legal problems, and so on. And this company will perform these services

every month, for the life of the business, for around $20 per year. ("It doesn't take any special knowledge to do it.")

- Provides expert consultants free of charge to train and personally advise you for an unlimited number of hours, for the life of the business.

"Ask them if they would consider it if all this were true," says Clements. "Most likely they'll say something like, 'Well, sure. But there's got to be a catch.'"

At this point, you tell them that network marketing provides all of the above. You've now completed Step A of the ABC process—suggesting to your prospect that network marketing is easier than starting *a conventional* business.

Step B is a little harder. Now you have to convince your prospect that network marketing is legitimate. Many distributors make the mistake here of flying into an impassioned defense of their industry, while heaping abuse on the mass media. This is overkill. Your prospect doesn't want to fight the establishment, and if she senses that that's your agenda, she'll probably lose interest. In most cases, when a prospect asks, "Isn't that an illegal pyramid scam?" she really just wants reassurance that what you're proposing is legal. The best and quickest way to provide this assurance is as follows: (1) to acknowledge that there have been many abuses of network marketing in the past, just as there have with franchising, real estate, stock market speculation, and every other form of business; and (2) to point out that network marketing is now 50 years old, has entered its third or mature wave of evolution, and is now being used by companies like Coca-Cola, Gillette, Colgate-Palmolive, and MCI.

Step C is the easiest. That's where you sell your particular product and opportunity. Use the presentation technique recommended by your upline sponsor.

STEP #3: ANSWER OBJECTIONS

If your prospect raises questions or objections during your ABC presentation, you should ask him to note them down, to be answered later.

"Let me finish making my whole point first," you could tell him, "and by the time I'm through, some of your questions may already have been answered."

"Ninety to ninety-five percent of all the 'objections' you get are the same ones that have been answered again and again by hundreds, even thousands of distributors," says John Kalench in *Being the Best You Can Be in MLM*.

The ABC technique is custom-designed to answer automatically many of these most common objections. Nevertheless, your prospect may still have a few legitimate questions left over at the end. Now it's time for you to make good on your promise. Kalench recommends a six-step approach for handling any objection.

According to Kalench, the first step in handling any objection is to listen. Hear out the objection in full. Don't interrupt. Don't cut her off. Don't assume that you know what she's going to say before she finishes saying it.

Secondly, transform the objection into a question. Most objections, according to Kalench, are either stalling tactics, to delay a decision, or questions in disguise. In many cases, your prospect may raise an objection that you think has already been addressed in your ABC presentation. Don't get annoyed. Don't say, "As I already explained to you . . ." That just insults your prospect.

When your prospect has finished stating her objection, transform it, in your mind, into a question. Kalench suggests you do this by adding the phrase, "Isn't that true?" at the end. For example, if your prospect says, "Oh, yeah, this is like one of those pyramid things I've heard about," tack on the question "Isn't that true?" and suddenly you realize that your prospect is really asking whether your business is legal—a very important and legitimate question. Suppose your prospect says, "I just don't have the time to do this." Add the phrase "Isn't that true?" and you see quite clearly that your prospect wants to know if she can make it in this business, even with limited time.

Now that you understand the true nature of your prospect's objection, acknowledge that she has raised a legitimate point. A good phrase to use is, "I appreciate what you're saying." Then pause. Don't use the word, "but." If you say, "I appreciate what you're saying, *but . . .*" that's just another way of saying, "I *don't* appreciate what you're saying."

Now answer the objection. Kalench warns against trying to smother your prospect's objections with facts. In most cases, your prospect already knows the facts, since she's already heard them in your ABC presentation. What she really wants is reassurance and encouragement. The best way to provide this, according to Kalench, is to tell a story from your own experience or that of someone you know.

For example, suppose your prospect says, "I don't think I'm really the sales type of personality." Tell her how you once had the same insecurity when you first got into network marketing. Relate some funny incident where you embarrassed yourself with your sales incompetence. Then tell how, with the help of your upline, and the duplicatable selling system of the Wave-Three organization you represent, you were able to transcend your own inadequacies and become a success.

By showing your imperfection and vulnerability, you build rapport with your prospect. And your story provides precisely the sort of reassurance she needs.

After telling the story, make sure it sunk in. Ask your prospect, "Does that make sense to you?" "Do you see how that could happen for you?" "Does that address your concern?"

The final step in Kalench's counter-objection system is to present your prospect with alternatives. If your prospect is still doubtful, you can take off some of the pressure by presenting her with a choice. Suppose her objection is that she has no time. Tell her, "Look, why don't you just try the product for a couple of weeks and see how you like it?" No matter what her objection, there will always be some alternative you can offer that will seem like a compromise.

STEP #4: APPLY PAIN AND PLEASURE

Psychologists agree that fear of pain is far more persuasive than desire for pleasure. But the most potent motivator of all is pain and pleasure combined. One of the surest ways to get your prospect thinking is to convince him that he will live to regret it if he fails to get into network marketing now. At the same time you can sweeten the threat by revealing further benefits of network marketing.

This is a hard sell. But if your prospect fails to yield to the ABC pitch, it's time to bring out the big guns.

Can You Retire Before You Die?

Sometimes, Yarnell uses pure fear as an incentive to join his downline. This approach is particularly effective during hard times like the present, when a lot of people are out of work. It can also be used on people who work hard for little income, such as teachers.

Yarnell's approach is to ask people, "Can you retire before you die?"

Most people will screw up their faces and squint at you in perplexity. That's the right response. Now restate the question.

"Will you be able to save enough money with your present income, so that you'll be able to afford to retire? Or will you just have to keep working till you die?"

Now you've got their attention. Point out to the prospect that, at the current 3-percent rate of inflation, a

35-year-old person making $60,000 today will be unable to retire at a similar standard of living. That's because, by the time that prospect turns 65 (in the year 2023) he'll have to earn $150,000 a year to buy what $60,000 would today.

"If you get 5-percent interest," says Yarnell, "that will require a nest egg of $3 million."

Your hapless prospect will have to sock away $43,915.66 a year, from this day forward. But if he's only making $60,000, that would be more than his entire net income, after taxes. It's obviously impossible.

That's when you pop the big question.

"How can you create nearly $100,000 in disposable annual income every year for the next three decades?"

In most cases, your prospect will be at a loss. Stock speculation, real estate, and other get-rich-quick mainstays of the last decade have all faded away. For most people, the only thing left is network marketing.

The "System" Pitch

So much for the pain. Now it's time to pour on more pleasure. Experience shows that the one thing your prospect wants to hear most is that the business will be easy to work. Without deceiving him, there's a lot you can say that will reinforce the idea that network marketing is easier than other businesses.

Never underestimate to your prospects the difficulty of working your business. It will only backfire on you later, as disgruntled distributors start blaming you for having led them down the garden path. You should always tell them exactly how much money it will probably cost, how much work it will take, and how many months it will probably be before they see top results.

Nevertheless, there are aspects of your Wave-Three business that make it easier to succeed at than conventional businesses. Emphasize those aspects. Sell your prospects on the power of the Wave-Three system, as well as on your company's training programs—the books, tapes, and videos available, the local training seminars offered in your prospect's area.

STEP #5: RELIEVE THE PRESSURE

Throughout your presentation, you must maintain a delicate balance between pressure and release. The best ways to relieve pressure are to keep reminding your prospect that there is a way out.

Always remember—this is a low-impact sale. Spice your every word and phrase with *impact subtractors* like "money-back guarantee" and "absolutely no obligation." Whenever you sense that your prospect is reacting negatively to the pressure, remind him or her that there are options requiring less money and effort than a fulltime commitment to the business, for instance, working the business part time. Sign on as a wholesale buyer. Or sell just enough to finance personal use of the product. And keep reminding your prospect that the company offers a money-back guarantee on all its products (as most reputable companies do).

STEP #6: APPLY SYNERGY

Perhaps the most powerful weapon in the Wave-Three persuasion arsenal is *synergy*. That's what happens when many parts or components work together, to create a force greater than the sum of its parts. In network marketing, the components are individual people. They act together in unison to generate an infectious excitement.

Satellite and teleconferences both tap into synergy. Much of their persuasive power comes from the invisible presence of a large viewing audience. Your prospect doesn't see that audience, but he knows it's there. A speakerphone meeting adds greater synergy, because the prospect hears the conference in the presence of other people.

But the greatest synergy of all still comes from that most traditional of network-marketing techniques—the live meeting. Whether a home meeting attended by a dozen people, or a national rally attended by thousands, the live meeting remains one of MLM's most powerful persuasive tools. If you aspire to upline leadership, you must become a master of live meetings.

The Party Plan

The classic MLM opportunity meeting is held in a hotel conference room, and attended by hundreds of people. Such events are expensive and difficult to set up. Until your organization is well-developed, leave such events to your upline. They have the money, the clout, and the experience to pull it off. Less experienced networkers who attempt hotel meetings often find themselves facing an expensive conference room filled with only a handful of their own distributors.

That's why most MLM trainers recommend that new distributors start out with home parties. Life Extension International distributor Sandy Elsberg suggests a staged approach to opportunity meetings, which I call the "party plan."

What Are Home Meetings For?

Just as at a big hotel meeting, your purpose at a home meeting is to present the product, the opportunity, and positive distributor testimony, to sign up new recruits, and to sell product. It also helps you train new distributors since your new recruits help you run the meeting and talk to the guests.

"A home meeting is easier to get to than a hotel," says Elsberg, "far less intimidating . . . warmer, cheaper, much more intimate, and—it doesn't send a conflicting message. There's something about showing up at a Holiday Inn with a whole pack of strangers after a hard day at the office that doesn't quite fit with all the promised freedoms of MLM."

How to Do a Home Meeting

One of the main selling points of a home party is its duplicatability. Everyone at the party should see how easy and fun it is to give one. They should be able to imagine themselves doing the same.

The refreshments shouldn't be too fancy. Don't waste your time with lavish decorations. Concentrate instead on creating a warm, homey atmosphere.

Have music playing. Serving alcohol is not advised. "No one will be offended if you don't serve alcohol," says trainer John Kalench, "But some may be offended if you do."

Above all, make your guests feel relaxed and at home.

Front End and Back End

Elsberg divides parties into a front end and back end. During the front end, you present the product and the company. On the back end, you present the compensation plan, talk about the market, and provide inspirational testimony and other motivation.

Division of Labor

To save wear and tear on yourself and your home, you should consider the hosting of home parties to be an obligation of your downline recruits. At the party, your downline acts as host or hostess, introduces you, and presents his or her own testimony.

"You bring all the literature, all the product, and any support material necessary to make the evening a success," says Elsberg.

The Presentation

The precise manner of your presentation will depend upon your product, your company, and the sort of people you are reaching out to. In this, as in all matters, the best advice is to defer to your upline. Your sponsor has done this many times and no doubt has an effective presentation already prepared. Don't reinvent the wheel.

Use a VCR

Make the fullest use you can of your company's recruiting videos. It appeals to the visually oriented among your guests, and it takes away much of the burden from the speaker. Elsberg recommends having a video going constantly while people are arriving at the party.

The Wrap-Up

After the presentation, make sure you leave time to work the crowd, writing out product orders and signing up new recruits. This is also a good time to invite everyone to next week's party, perhaps with a flyer announcing time, place, and special guest.

"Your guest could be someone who lost 100 pounds with your products or a great financial testimony," suggests Elsberg.

Three by Three

Elsberg recommends a three-by-three approach to building your business through parties. Sponsor your partygivers-in-training by couples. If you sponsor a married couple, that's perfect. But if your recruit is single, pair him or her up with a buddy, so they can work as a team. You and your pair of trainees form the threesome. This gives you more leverage for your training efforts, since you're now training two partygivers for the effort of training one.

Your goal is to recruit three teams of partygivers and work with them simultaneously, setting aside a different weekday night for each team to give its party.

Four-Week Training

Each team will need four weeks of training before being cut loose. Each week, that team will give another party. After doing one party with a new pair, ask which of them would like to volunteer to put on half of the next party. Let that person do the front half, which is the easier half, while you take the back end. On week three, you remove yourself from the process and let your trainees run the show. The one who did the front end of the meeting during week two is now promoted to doing the back end, while his or her partner does the front end. Your only job during week three will be to introduce the testimony portion, and close the meeting.

Week four is graduation week. You still attend the meeting. But your team handles every aspect themselves. You're only there to provide encouragement and praise.

Party Momentum

Your party machine will keep growing three by three. After taking three teams through the four-week training cycle, take on another three teams. Each team, when it finishes training, becomes the frontline leadership of a separate party leg of your organization—a leg that can give its own parties independently.

"They've learned how to give presentations," says Elsberg, "how to make three-way calls, how to tell their story, how to retail, how to recruit, sponsor, and teach . . . and each of these legs has 20–30 people—maybe 50."

According to Elsberg, once you have six party legs in your downline, you've achieved *party momentum*. You're ready to give your first hotel meeting.

WHY THE BIG MEETING?

Many Wave-Three pioneers look down their noses at hotel meetings today. They see them as old-fashioned relics of a previous era. They believe that people today don't have time for meetings. They're wary of the carnival atmosphere, the revival-style testimonials, the air of razzle-dazzle. Many of today's most up-to-date networkers feel far more comfortable working behind the low-impact smoke-screen of endless videos, teleconferences, and satellite broadcasts.

But the power that big hotel meetings offer is the same as it was from the earliest days of Nutrilite. And, to this day, no one has thought of an effective methodology that fully duplicates its synergy.

The Party Before the Party

First impressions are the strongest. Your guests should feel the full impact of your meeting from the first moment they walk in the door. Elsberg calls this moment the "party before the party."

"When they walk inside, it's a party!" she says. "The music is hot, the people are networking, and everyone is

helping everyone else feel welcome and comfortable. Someone is getting you a drink . . . someone else is adding more
chairs... someone else takes you up to the product display.
There are posters and balloons everywhere, and you have a
lot of humor and fun happening."

The Registration Table

Your guests will get their first impression from your registration table, which should be set up right outside the
meeting room. Elsberg suggests covering the table with a
linen tablecloth and festooning it with balloons and con-
fetti. If your company has gotten a recent write-up in the
press, blow up the article, and display it prominently on an
easel. Each guest should be given a reprint of the article,
along with their other literature.

John Kalench advises staffing your registration table
with happy, outgoing people, to make a positive first impression. At the table, take everyone's name, address, and
phone number and provide every attendee with a color-
coded name tag, the color distinguishing between associates of your company and new guests.

Atmospherics

As in a home meeting, from the moment your guests enter,
they should never be allowed to feel bored or neglected. There
could be lively music playing, to lend excitement. Work the
crowd hard, making it a point to meet with every new guest,
recognizable by their colored name tags. Instruct your frontline leaders to do the same, and pass the word on down the
line. Unless your downline distributors have specific instructions to work the crowd, they may tend to treat the meeting
as a social get-together and congregate with their own clique.
During the meeting, upline leaders should circulate around,

keeping an eye on their downlines and making sure people are focusing on guests, not on one another.

The Chair Trick

Another important atmospheric effect is that all through the party—at least the first portion—guests should be subliminally aware of chairs being constantly added to the room. This generates the impression that the meeting's attendance is exceeding expectations. Actually, in a well-planned meeting, you should deliberately set out fewer chairs than the number of guests you expect. There's nothing worse than empty chairs, but few things more positive than the constant clamor of adding new chairs for a swelling audience.

Product Display

The product display in the back of the room should be a center of energy. If your product is an easily sampled food item, give out free samples. This should cause people to line up.

The display itself should be impressive, professional, and interesting. Don't skimp. Fill it with props, charts, graphs, and company literature.

The Presentation

John Kalench recommends that the first speaker should go on for 20–30 minutes and should probably not be a superstar. Your guests need to see someone they can relate to, not some multimillionaire. It's better to have a new distributor who's attained some modest success.

The presentation should introduce the network-marketing industry, the company, products, and the opportunity.

Kalench suggests it be followed by 45 minutes of distributor testimony, all designed to answer five crucial questions:

- Is this business simple?
- Can I have fun doing it?
- Can I make money doing it?
- Will they help me do it?
- Is the timing perfect for me to get involved now?

Just as at the home party, you should leave time afterward for you and your downline to work the crowd.

Special Guest by Speakerphone

Elsberg suggests bringing in a special guest by speakerphone during the meeting. This helps you involve prominent personalities, like your company president, who wouldn't otherwise have the time to attend. The novelty of it also adds an air of excitement.

It makes people feel important," says Elsberg, "that somewhere out there, this important person is calling in, right now, to talk to us!"

No Down-Time

Pacing is crucial.

"You don't want any down time," says Elsberg, "no clumsy gaps where one piece is finished but the next one hasn't started."

This is particularly important during the testimony phase, when you'll have a score of people taking the podium one after the other.

"Make this into a testimony parade!" Elsberg advises. "Have your people trained to be up and moving the moment the parade begins . . . no details, hit the high points, one or two minutes max, one after the other."

Strength in Numbers

Motivational author W. Clement Stone once wrote that the best sort of money to use in a business endeavor is OPM— Other People's Money.

Network marketers go two steps beyond that, says Sandy Elsberg. They use OPT (other people's time, talent, and technique) and OPE (other people's energy, education, and enthusiasm). In short, they use people power. Other people are your greatest resource in network marketing.

A parade of testimonials at a meeting will persuade more readily than a self-serving sales pitch from one person. A huge, nationwide organization will impress far more deeply than one distributor with a video. The sheer numbers of people involved in your business amplifies your persuasive force by showing your prospect that you are not alone. Teleconferences, speakerphone parties, home and hotel meetings—indeed, the entire panoply of Wave-Three persuasion techniques have been expertly crafted to enable you to leverage the people power, the strength of numbers residing in your company. Stick with the system, follow the procedures, and you will never face a prospect without an army of unseen allies at your back.

SECTION 3

OPPORTUNITY

Chapter 8

WAVE-THREE SPONSORING

"Stick with your upline and stay away from other leaders," cautioned Mark Yarnell, "until you're making about $50,000 a year."

Kathy Denison was puzzled by her sponsor's warning. Why did she have to stay away from other leaders? What was so dangerous about them? Although she didn't understand it, Denison nevertheless stuck to her sponsor's advice. It was only months later that she discovered the wisdom in it.

Denison had moved to California. Her sponsor was now a thousand miles away. She was surrounded by strangers. The first time Denison walked into an opportunity meeting, she was stunned.

"One of the Blue Diamond distributors was giving a speech at a hotel," says Denison, "and he said that the only way you're going to be successful in this business is if you get people to buy five kits—about $1,500 worth of product—when they sign up."

Denison had learned an entirely different approach from Yarnell. She sold new prospects only a single starter kit for about $150.

"I suddenly thought, 'Oh my God, I'm on the wrong path!'" says Denison.

But her panic was shortlived. Denison found that Yarnell's method worked just as well in California as it had in Colorado. And, despite the dire warnings of her local leaders, Denison's business continued to thrive.

"Everybody's got a different way to do the business," Denison concludes. "Everybody has their own opinion."

FOLLOW YOUR SPONSOR'S SYSTEM

Sponsoring is an art, not a science. There's no single formula that works for everybody, all the time. However, 50 years of trial and error in network marketing have yielded one rock-bottom principle from which no one should deviate:

You must work your sponsor's system—whatever it is.

"When you're first in the business," says Denison, "you're on a learning curve. And it's easier to stick with one way to do the business. When you start reading other people's training manuals and listening to other people's tapes, it confuses you. You start thinking 'I'm not doing this right and I'm not doing that right.' You start judging yourself. It's overwhelming."

In the beginning, do it your sponsor's way. Only after completing your apprenticeship should you dare to experiment. In Yarnell's system, that means after you're making $50,000 a year from your network-marketing business.

"At that point," says Denison, "you can do whatever you want."

Trust the System

But how do you know that your sponsor's advice is correct?

You don't, exactly. But you've got to trust the system. If your sponsor were completely incompetent, the system would have purged him long ago. Your sponsor's personal system may not be the best. But it works. And, with all its imperfections, following it will get you to your goal a lot faster than wasting time, money, and energy trying to reinvent the wheel.

The Power of Humility

Terry Hill had to swallow a lot of pride before she became truly teachable. As Xerox Corporation's top salesperson, Hill was used to doing business in sleek offices and five-star restaurants. So when she drove up for her first meeting with Mark Yarnell, she was startled to see that the address he'd given her was a small private home in a not-so-affluent neighborhood. Hill almost turned around and drove away. In fact, the only reason she didn't was that another car pulled up behind her and blocked her way! She decided to go in and meet the guy anyway.

Yarnell at that time was a penniless minister who had turned to network marketing when his preaching failed to pay the bills. But Hill sensed that he knew MLM better than she did. She became his student.

"In MLM, everyone starts at the bottom," says Hill. "It's a very humbling experience."

Hill calls the first six months of her Nu Skin business "one of the most devastating times of my life." As hard as she tried, she couldn't seem to match the income she'd had at Xerox. In despair, she called Yarnell.

"What's wrong with me?" she pleaded.

Yarnell told her to unlearn all her high-powered sales skills. At Xerox, Hill had been known as an aggressive, high-pressure closer. Those were important skills when you were selling expensive laserprinters to major companies and every sale was worth millions. But in network marketing, it didn't help to close a sale—that is, to recruit a new distributor—if the next day or the next week, your new recruit decided to drop out.

"It was really a lifestyle decision I was selling," says Hill. "It's very personal. And the only thing that really works is if your prospect believes in the product and the opportunity."

Yarnell's approach was the opposite of Hill's. He put no pressure on prospects and spent very little time with them. He showed up for appointments in jeans, presented the opportunity in 45 minutes, then left his phone number. Those who called back were the ones he wanted.

Once Hill learned the knack, she was on easy street. Within a year and a half, she'd surpassed her former income at Xerox. Today, she and her husband are millionaires. And she did it all by following the advice of a down-and-out back-country preacher.

Sponsoring: The Real Work of Wave Three

Sponsorship is the real work of network marketing. Wave-Three systems and technology have long since stolen most other functions from human hands. Company computers handle your paperwork and product orders. Videos and teleconferences take the grind out of prospecting. What does that leave for you to do?

"All the tools and technology free you up to focus on that one most intangible part of this business," says John Fogg, editor of *Upline,* "which is relationships with people. Your job is to develop your people and support them in building their business."

The Turnkey Approach

Does that mean that a network marketer must be a gifted teacher, mentor, and leader, in order to succeed? What if you're shy? Uncommunicative? More of a listener than a talker? Unsure of your knowledge? How can you presume to teach others, when you're not sure how much you know yourself?

Wave Three strikes again!

Even in this last frontier of strictly human endeavor, systems and technology have combined to create a low-impact approach, streamlined, simplified, and accessible to the most average distributor.

"What you've got in network marketing," says John Fogg, "is a turnkey operation, where a new distributor can come in, turn the key, drive right off, and be in business."

Boiled down to its bare essentials, an upline sponsor does two things—makes presentations and answers questions from downline distributors. Wave-Three systems have rendered both of these tasks a lot easier.

"There's training that needs to be done, but it's a heck of a lot less than to run a McDonald's," says Fogg. "You've got a duplicatable business system that Richard can give to Mark, who can give it to Sally, and so on. You focus on developing those individuals as leaders rather than on managing them."

Leadership in a Can

In short, you don't have to wait to be a wise old sage before you can start imparting your wisdom to your disciples. In a Wave-Three organization, you sponsor in stages, teaching your downline only what you yourself have learned so far.

Indeed, as Fogg points out, you really start sponsoring someone the moment you offer your product at retail. Let's say you're selling a weight-loss product. Your prospect tries it and loses weight.

"Has anybody at work commented on your weight loss?" you ask. "Have you told them about the product? "

There it is. Lesson number one. You've already begun to teach the three-foot rule, and the fundamentals of prospecting through retail sales.

Let's say your prospect already has five or six people at this point who want the product. Most prospects will react by saying, "I'll give you their names so you can sell them the products."

That's your cue to start sponsoring your prospect on to the next level of achievement.

"That's great," you say. "Thanks for the referrals. But let me suggest something. Why don't you give those names to yourself? You can get the products at wholesale for your own use, retail them to these people, and put the money in your pocket. In essence, you'll get your product for free."

Lesson number two is now in the can. You've helped your prospect see how easy it really is to get in business as a distributor.

Fogg calls this method *backing them into the business*. Before they know what's happened, they're sitting dutifully at your feet, awaiting your next instructions.

THE MASTERY PRINCIPLE

Only when your recruits have completely mastered one step of the business should you move them on to the next.

Let's say your prospect uses only $50 worth of product per month of your nutritional product. And let's say he retails another $50 worth to one or two people that he knows. That's $100 per month.

"Do $100 per month for a month or two," says Fogg, "and you could easily say that you've mastered that step of the business."

Now move your recruit to the next step. Teach him to become a sponsor. He already knows everything there is to know about moving $100 per month. Now let him teach other people to do exactly the same thing.

From this moment on, your recruit is building his frontline. Let's say you belong to a company in which you become a five-star executive by recruiting five frontline leaders. Your recruits' goal then should be to recruit five people each and teach them to move $100 worth of product each month.

Once he's done that, your recruit will now have a monthly personal volume of $600. After doing that for a couple of months, he will have mastered it. Now he teaches his five recruits to do the same. How do they do it? The same way he did. They use $100 worth of product themselves and get five people to move $100 per month.

So now your recruit has five people doing $600 volume per month. That gives him a personal volume of $3,600 per month. After maintaining that level for a couple of months, he's mastered it. He can now teach each of his five leaders to do the same. And on it goes.

FIVE LEADERS

As your organization grows, it will fill up with part-timers, wholesale buyers, and people who just don't want to work. Pay no attention to them. Focus your time and energy on your frontline leaders—those people whom you personally recruited and personally sponsor.

The optimum number of leaders in your frontline will depend upon your compensation plan. But, in general, five is considered the maximum you can personally sponsor with effectiveness. If each of those five sponsors five other leaders, training them in accordance with the mastery principle, your downline will grow like wildfire.

GO WIDE

Experienced networkers say your frontline is never wide enough. You should keep recruiting frontline leaders, long after you have your five leaders in place. That's because you really don't know how each trainee is going to work out until months down the line. Some may look good in the beginning, but lack persistence and drop out later. Others may defect to another company. Still others may quarrel with you, or slack off because of personal problems.

To find one good leader, you must sift through scores of prospects. It's better to pursue this long-term, tedious process on an ongoing basis, rather than resort to it in an emergency when you experience sudden losses in your frontline.

BUILD A LEADER EVERY 30 DAYS

In order to focus your efforts most effectively, Big Al recommends training your leaders one at a time. Every 30 days, you move on to train a new leader.

Start by selecting your most promising frontline distributor and making this offer: "If you want to be a leader, I'm willing to be your full-time employee for at least one month, or until you reach the leader level."

Then follow through. There's a lot you can do in 30 days to help your trainee experience immediate results. Among them are the following:

Two-on-One

The first thing you need to do as your trainee's full-time employee is commit to doing two-on-ones any time of the day or night. During those 30 days, never let your trainee make her sales pitches solo. Insist that she bring all her prospects to you, either in a three-way phone call or a two-on-one meeting. Then present the opportunity exactly as your sponsor presented it in your three-ways.

Turbocharge Your Prospect's Downline

During the 30 days, all your leads and prospects will go into your trainee's downline. Nothing will excite and inspire your trainee more than watching her downline grow.

Train Your Prospect's Recruits

Help her recruits with two-on-ones, prospecting leads, and home meetings.

Lend Your Own Upline

Set aside two days per week, during which you and your trainee will work full time with *your* sponsor.

Buy Advertising

Either you or your sponsor may wish to invest a few hundred dollars to take out ads for your trainee in a local newspaper.

THE COLD, HARD CASH EFFECT

"Nothing motivates better," says Big Al, "than helping people reach their goals."

Sales leaders in many fields have long understood that the best way to get people's attention is to show them that they will make more money if they do things your way.

Armstrong Williams once had a distributor named Nancy who was unable to convince a single person to cough up the $35 distributor fee for Dick Gregory's Bahamian

Diet. Nancy tried everything. Finally, she was ready to quit in despair.

Many sponsors would have labeled Nancy a "problem person" and let her go. They would have saved their time and energy for their more promising heavy hitters. But Williams believed in Nancy and wanted her to win.

"I said, 'Take me out with you,'" says Williams. "Let me go with you, and let's make it work."

At the very first sales call, Williams spotted the problem. When she gave her presentation, Nancy was not looking people in the eye.

"Most people feel that if a person can't look them in the eye, they can't be trusted," says Williams.

Of course, Nancy was eminently trustworthy. But she was shy. Williams made her practice maintaining eye contact until it became second nature. Then he went with her on ten sales calls, in which he personally signed up ten people into Nancy's downline, just to reinforce to her that it could be done.

Nancy got the message. Not only did she go on to succeed, but she became Williams' top performer!

In the same way, Big Al's 30-day plan is certain to put money in the pockets of each trainee who goes through it. As the other frontline distributors watch what's happening, they'll soon be champing at the bit for their turn.

Work Backwards

When you set goals for your trainees, John Fogg recommends that you work backwards.

Let's say that your trainee wants to make $50,000 a year in two years. That's your target. Now go backwards to the present time, setting up regular milestones along the way, which you judge to be realistic according to your compensation plan.

For example, if your trainee needs to have twelve breakaway leaders to achieve a first-year subgoal of $25,000, that means one leader per month will do the trick. Recruiting one leader thus becomes your goal for the 30-day intensive training period.

Leadership Momentum

All of your downline members don't need to be leaders, and they won't be. But without a few committed big fish, you're always going to be playing catch-up in your business.

One leader in your downline can yield hundreds of times the sales volume of a score of half-hearted part-timers. Moreover, leaders are committed to your downline. They've sunk a lot of their own time and money into building the business and will not be so quick to jump ship as your other distributors.

PUT YOUR DOWNLINE ON AUTOPILOT

With enough leaders in your downline, you can put your business on autopilot. Trained leaders can be trusted to run your meetings for you and to keep the prospecting momentum going while you disappear for a few weeks to the Bahamas. In short, the number and quality of your leaders directly controls the amount of time freedom you can ultimately draw from your business.

The 3-30-300 Principle

Perhaps the greatest enemy of your time freedom is the phenomenon that David Roller calls the 3-30-300 Principle. According to this universal law of distributor behavior, your downline's demands for attention will tend to monopolize 100 percent of your time and energy, regardless of whether your organization consists of 3, 30, or 300 people! Unless you fight back with conscious stratagems, you will soon be reduced to abject slavery, an overworked scullery maid at the beck and call of your every downline master or mistress.

"You cannot be everything to everyone," says Roller. "You will need to make decisions on where it is best to invest your time."

Prioritize Your Efforts

The simplest and most powerful technique for winning back your life is to prioritize your downline trainees.

Roller suggests listing the names and phone numbers of every distributor whom you personally sponsor. The list should be in some easily edited format. For example, you can write them in pencil, on small Post-Its, or, best of all, on a computer or word processor.

Now, arrange the names in order, starting from your most active distributors, by monthly volume. The closer to the top they are, the more worthy of your attention. When you play back your voice-mail messages each day, use this list to determine who gets a call back and how long you'll stay on the phone with each person.

The list should be updated at least once a month.

Speak in Info Bursts

Answering questions is one of your most important and time-consuming duties as an upline leader. Yet, many of your answers are wasted because they are too long and complicated. The questioner just sloughs it off and probably comes back in a few days to ask the same question over again.

Learn to speak in *info bursts*.

Train yourself to answer questions as succinctly as possible. Make it a game. With every phone call, challenge yourself to dispense with each question and get the questioner off the phone as quickly as possible. As you gain practice, you'll be surprised how little information you really need in order to wrap up each call.

Also, be wary of irrelevant questions. If your trainee lures you off on some abstract subject, gently but firmly steer him back toward the real subject—how to get practical results from his downline now.

Traffic Control

As your downline grows, the demands upon your time will grow ever more intense. Suddenly, you have more phone calls than you can handle. Your monthly printout is filled with strangers' names. People in other states are besieging you with requests to sponsor them, to answer their questions, to fly out and conduct meetings for them. Your phone becomes an information bottleneck with incoming and outgoing calls colliding in a nerve-wracking mass of call-waiting bleeps and breathless interruptions from self-important strangers who want you to drop what you're doing and take their call right now.

In short, your information flow is out of control.

Wave-Three technology offers some surprising solutions to the problem of traffic control. One of the most powerful is voice mail. When used creatively, this simple device can transform your telephone bottleneck into an Information superhighway.

Who's the Boss?

Who's the boss? You or your telephone?

In the past, upline leaders jumped at every ring of the phone, like trained dogs at their master's command. Con-

ventional answering machines provided only the illusion of
control. In practice, leaders with answering machines would
typically drop what they were doing and screen each incoming call. And unless they wanted to install half a dozen new
phone lines, they had to put up with a constant bombardment of call-waiting bleeps right in the midst of their most
soul-searching conversations with frontline leaders. Of
course, you could ignore the bleep. But then you'd spend the
rest of your life wondering if the caller you missed was that
big fish who might have put you on Easy Street.

Voice Processing

Voice mail, on the other hand, puts you in total control. You
control your information flow as precisely and deliberately
as you manipulate characters on your word-processing
screen.

A voice-mail system takes messages all day and all
night, without intrusive ringing. Messages can be as long
as necessary. And your voice mailbox will keep recording
incoming messages even while you're on the other line conducting a two-hour phone training session with one of your
frontline leaders.

Good voice-mail systems will allow you to save or
delete particular messages, to rewind and fast forward, or
do a quick check that lets you hear the first few seconds of
each message. Some services offer a Help! option, similar
to those that guide computer illiterates through the rudi-
ments of new software.

"Let's say somebody leaves me a message telling me a
great story about how they've used a particular book in
their organization," says John Mann, a distributor for Kla-
math Falls, OR-based CellTech. "I can pull out that message from the rest and broadcast it to ten of my key leaders,
and they can hear the testimonial in the person's own
words, instead of my having to repeat it all over again."

Use Communication Clusters

Voice mail users can structure their working days around what Glen Davidson of Concord Communications calls "communication clusters."

A communication cluster is a specific time that you set aside each day for interacting by phone. You listen to the messages in your voice mailbox and respond to the most important or urgent of them. The rest of the day, you don't even think about the phone. While you engage in personal meetings, brainstorming, or other activities, your voice mailbox fills up with messages.

If one of your downline calls in with a question better answered by one of your frontline leaders, just push a button, and that message will be forwarded to the appropriate person.

And if you only need to give a simple yes or no answer to someone's question, simply call her voice mailbox and say "yes" or "no." You don't have to fear being caught up in a prolonged, impromptu discussion just because you happen to have caught your voice-mail correspondent at a talkative moment.

Build Techno-Relationships

One of voice mail's most potent uses is to create *techno-relationships*—personal interactions that would never have existed without electronic intervention. Network marketing is a people-to-people business. Your bottom line depends upon the *quality* and *quantity* of your human contacts. When put to work in a Wave-Three network, voice mail enhances both.

John Mann was a gifted concert cellist and composer. But by age 26, he concluded that music wasn't paying his bills.

"I vowed that I would quit professional composing until I had the financial clout to make my own recordings and call my own shots," he says. "I'm finally achieving that long-term dream, at age 40."

Today, Mann has over 12,000 people in his CellTech downline. He ascribes much of his newfound success and freedom to his *techno-relationships*. A natural tinkerer, Mann confesses a lifelong weakness for gadgets and gizmos.

"As a professional musician, I was used to experimenting with new ways to communicate through physical instruments," he says. "I'm fascinated by the way technology allows ordinary people to do the extraordinary."

Yet even a techie like Mann was dumbfounded when his sponsor first told him about voice mail.

"I couldn't figure out what he was talking about," says Mann. "I couldn't picture it. I didn't get it."

Like most people, Mann thought voice mail was just a souped-up answering machine. But after going online, Mann found that he had entered a new world.

Among some American Indian tribes, a "talking stick" is passed around in council. Whoever holds the stick is entitled to speak, without interruption. Mann calls voice mail an "electronic talking stick," which improves human interaction in ways that its inventors could never have foreseen.

When someone in your downline leaves an extended message on your voice mail box, you must listen to every word, without interrupting. Conversations can last for days. Your distributors can tell you exactly what's on their minds, with one phone call. They don't get a busy signal, a broken answering machine, or a harried voice saying, "I'm on the other line, I'll call you back later."

Through voice mail, Mann built a techno-relationship with his top producer, a distributor on his third level, whom Mann barely knew.

"We started exchanging voice-mail messages," says Mann. "Over six months, message after message, we became more familiar, swapping personal stories. It's like sitting on a long bus ride with somebody. We really got to know each other. He's one of my best friends now. Through voice mail."

Voice mail "cross-fertilizes" downlines, according to Mann, causing distributors in widely different "legs" of an organization to exchange data on training programs, technological innovations, new books and tapes available, and even to share inspiring testimonials.

"It produced much more alignment of purpose and shared experience in our company," said Mann. "And that translates directly into more sales."

Interactive Roundtables

Mann advises using voice mail to create interactive roundtables with your downline. Let's say you need to discuss an important issue. You send a voice-mail broadcast to your six frontline leaders, describing the problem in detail, and requesting responses within 24 hours. Your three-minute message will cost less than a dollar. Their responses may total three or four dollars on your phone bill. Even after going back and forth this way for a couple of days, your entire conference will probably not exceed $10 in cost. That's a lot cheaper than a standard conference call or a physical meeting, involving heavy costs in time, travel, and hotel bills.

Wave-Three Newsletters

Upline leaders have long used newsletters as a management tool. They keep downline distributors abreast of company news, publicize success stories, and provide a forum for upline leaders to exhort the troops. A free subscription to your newsletter also makes a nice premium to offer your new prospects.

But quality newsletters are tough and expensive to produce. Typesetting and printing bills alone provide an impenetrable cost barrier for most people, not to mention mailing costs.

However, more and more companies and upline leaders are offering voice-mail newsletters to their downlines. Once or twice a month, your downline gets a full news update and pep talk on their mailboxes. It may cost you $2 to transmit the whole thing.

Of course, the computer literate may choose to avail themselves of desktop publishing technology for the same purpose. John Mann used his Macintosh to spit out a monthly newsletter and distribute it to an elite group of 200 leaders in his downline, via fax broadcast.

"Those 200 leaders in turn disseminated it to their people," says Mann. "The newsletter was supposed to persuade wholesale buyers to become distributors. It worked. Within two months after I started doing that newsletter regularly, my group's dollar volume increased by about 30 percent."

The Automated Networker

CellTech's Mann is a pioneer in applying PCs to network marketing. He uses accounting software to compute profit and loss statements. He employs integrated software to instantly transfer names back and forth between daily planner, prospect file, and Rolodex. He sends out mailings by merged letters, customizing each letter for hundreds or even thousands of distributors or prospects. And his databases allow him to target mailings to selected subgroups, for example, everyone in his downline who hasn't reordered product in the past couple of months.

"I placed an ad that drew over 60 responses, and each one of those people got a typed, personal letter," says Mann, "courtesy of a mail-merged and ever-so-slightly customized letter. How much better results do you think I got than I would have gotten with a photocopied form letter?"

The PC Gap

Of course, in the Wave-Three organization, the proper place for computer hardware is back at the home office. Individual distributors don't waste a lot of their time fooling around with modems and disk drives.

Nevertheless, as computers become cheaper and simpler to use, a PC revolution will inevitably sweep network marketing. Even today, many upline leaders make ingenious use of PCs to do what upline leaders do best—sponsor other leaders.

For the average distributor, the $2,000 worth of equipment, as well as the time and effort required to master new software still present a barrier against "booting up" to Info-Age networking. But the PC gap is closing fast. In the near future, Wave-Three companies will likely offer software and online services as readily as they offer more traditional inducements to their distributors.

And Wave-Three leaders will continue to invent newer and better ways to employ that technology in sponsoring and training better leaders.

THE MEANING OF MASTERY

Your success or failure in network marketing ultimately depends upon your ability to create self-sufficient leaders. In the Wave-Three era, that doesn't mean maverick entrepreneurs, with overblown egos and oodles of talent. It means people who trust the system enough to follow it— even when you're not standing over their shoulders to make sure they follow the rules.

In no other field of endeavor does that old saw better apply, "In order to lead, you must first learn to follow."

The Wave-Three distributor must stifle his ego and harness his creativity in a system that may seem, on the surface, ridiculously simple. The distributor becomes a master only when he or she learns to appreciate the decades of trial and error that have gone into formulating that system, only when he or she is wise enough to use the company's existing procedures without trying to reinvent them.

Chapter 9

THE FIFTH INCOME STREAM

Howard Solomon was a heavy hitter.

During the days when National Safety Associates (NSA) was the hottest, fastest-growing company in MLM, Solomon was one of its top distributors, with a downline tens of thousands strong. While the money rolled in, Solomon and his wife flew all over the country, inspiring others with their stunning success story.

Most people in the industry would have considered Solomon the ultimate network marketer. But Solomon realizes today that he had some serious blind spots. Like most network marketers, Solomon assumed that there were only four ways to make money in MLM—wholesale commissions, retail commissions, overrides, and bonuses.

Not so!

The Wave-Three revolution has opened a fifth income stream—perhaps even more highly leveraged than the traditional ones. And you don't even need to be a distributor to access it.

CATCH THE WAVE

Today, network marketing exerts an invisible impact on capital markets around the world. As Wave Three deepens and matures, its impact will grow exponentially. Savvy investors will make millions by catching the wave of fast-growing MLM companies, not only through hands-on involvement as a distributor, but also through the stock market.

The astute investor can make a killing by following the chain of hidden influences that emanate through global capital markets, like ripples through a pond, from any successful network-marketing rollout.

Howard Solomon learned that lesson the hard way.

Play Your Hunches

You've heard of the seven-year itch. Howard Solomon had something even more aggravating. He had a seven-year hunch.

Back in the mid-1980s, Solomon was a small business owner. His company sold, installed, and monitored burglar-alarm systems. It was a good business. Solomon lived comfortably. His payroll wavered between 6 and 12 employees. But deep down inside, Solomon knew he was in a rut.

"I was never able to break through that glass ceiling," he admits, "and to achieve that quality of life and freedom that is such an elusive dream for us all."

Part of the problem, Solomon knew, was that his product was too expensive. The wireless burglar alarms he sold were state-of-the-art. They required no hardwiring, and they were designed to go off before the burglar broke through the door—not afterwards, when it might be too late. All that technology cost money. Solomon's alarm systems ran from $2,000–$3,000 a pop.

"It was out of reach of the masses," says Solomon. "The market was very limited. I said to myself that if some company could mass market a similar system for under $1,000, it would own the industry."

But Solomon didn't believe he was the man to do it. He didn't have the money. He didn't have a factory. He didn't have the know-how. He was just an average, small businessman. With a shrug and a sigh, Solomon tried to forget about his hunch.

Watch with an Eagle's Eye

Network marketers are a breed apart. Like an eagle surveying the land from his clifftop eyrie, the observant networker can often use his peculiar vantage point to discern trends and possibilities hidden to the conventional business world.

Solomon never expected to become a network marketer. Like most proper, small business owners, he held the industry in some disdain. But one day, a business acquaintance took Solomon aside and issued him a challenge.

"He said, 'I'll put my monthly check on the table and you put your monthly check on the table, and if my check is greater than yours, will you give me an hour to listen to what I have to say?'"

Solomon agreed. When he saw the figure on the other man's check, he practically choked.

"My ego went into my back pocket real quick," says Solomon. "And I listened."

The man was a distributor for National Safety Associates (NSA), a company that marketed water filters. Solomon was a distributor from that day forward. He rose quickly to the top. For the next four years, Solomon lived the high-powered life he'd never been able to achieve as a small-business owner. He sold off his burglar-alarm business without a second thought. He'd finally become a success.

But now and then, Solomon still found his old hunch returning to haunt him. "Just when *will* some entrepreneur bring out an affordable wireless alarm system?" Solomon would find himself wondering at odd moments. "And how much money will he really make?"

As long as Solomon was a conventional retailer, these remained idle speculations. It was his involvement with network marketing that ultimately opened his eyes and his ears to the biggest opportunity of his life.

The Magic of Duplication

The world is filled with dreamers like Solomon—people with multimillion-dollar ideas who never quite get around to implementing them. In the conventional business world, such people are discarded and ignored. Some eager beaver always comes along and beats them to the punch. Only those rare souls, in whom the proper blend of drive, money, genius, and opportunity converge ultimately bring the big ideas to market. The dreamers spend the rest of their lives wondering, "What if . . . ?"

But it is the peculiar magic of network marketing that a dreamer like Howard Solomon needn't surrender his dream simply because someone else beat him to market. The law of duplication ensures that one man's dream can be shared by another and another and another . . .

Seize the Moment

Solomon's big chance came in 1992. A bigtime network marketer approached Solomon about a new company called Quorum International. As a well-known heavy hitter, Solomon was used to fending off pitches from every new company that came along. But this time was different. To his amazement, Solomon heard that Quorum sold wireless security systems—for a few hundred dollars apiece.

"It was like déjà vu," Solomon remembers. "Here were all the pieces that I was looking for."

Solomon took a leap of faith. He left his cushy position at NSA and joined the fledgling company.

"It was the best business decision I ever made."

Today, Quorum has become one of the fastest-rising stars in network marketing, with 1993 sales projected at $250 million and over 300,000 distributors in its downline.

Solomon feels right at home with the product.

"I understand the technology," he says, "I understand the consumer mindset, and I certainly understand the potential in the marketplace."

On his own, Solomon probably would have gone the rest of his life doing nothing about his brilliant hunch. But as a Quorum distributor, he became a leader in a transnational industry of which Solomon was once among the smallest and humblest cogs. His Quorum downline today is 60,000 strong. No mere sales reps, Solomon and his wife Marie are integrally involved in plotting company strategy.

"We've been very instrumental in helping develop Quorum," says Solomon, "and we're among the top earners in the company today."

20/20 HINDSIGHT

So, with all that success, why is Solomon so rueful today?

Because he overlooked the power of the fifth income stream.

"I had blinders on," Solomon admits. "I was really focused 200 percent on building my Quorum business."

What Solomon failed to appreciate was the magnitude of Quorum's impact on a little-known manufacturer headquartered in . . . Hong Kong!

Hong Kong-based Applied Electronics owned 70 percent of Quorum International. And it manufactured 100 percent of Quorum's products. For years, Applied Electronics had produced everything from calculators and computer

parts to toys and games for multinational corporations like
Texas Instruments and IBM, who wished to avail themselves of cheap Hong Kong labor. But it was a minor company in a very minor market. Its stock, listed on the Hong
Kong exchange, sold for pennies per share. Only the most
careful observers of Pacific Rim business even noticed that
Applied Electronics existed.

In a little over a year, as a direct result of Quorum's
phenomenal growth in America, Applied Electronics' stock
multiplied ten times in value.

"I made some money on it," says Solomon. "But, hind-
sight being 20/20, I should have invested a lot more. If I
had it to do over again, I would mortgage the house, the
kids, the dog, and put everything into Applied stock."

Inside Trading

Solomon was like most people. His idea of stock-market
speculation was salting away a small portion of his savings
in blue-chip stocks. But now he's learned a valuable lesson.
He's learned that network marketers can use their eagle's
eyrie to spy unusual opportunities invisible to conventional
stock analysts.

"The best way to invest in network marketing," says
Solomon, "is to be part of a company on the growing curve.
Because I was in Quorum, I saw the tremendous growth it
was having. I could foresee the impact it was going to have
on Applied Electronics. It would be hard to see that if you
were outside the industry."

MLM Companies Going Public

As network marketing infiltrates the conventional business world, it creates hot investment opportunities where
before none existed. Take Rexall. Founded in 1903, Rexall

is a household name, recognized in 75 percent of American households. Rexall's drugstores once dotted the landscape.

But the company fell on hard times. In 1985, the Sundown vitamin company bought the trademark. Now called Rexall Sundown, the venerable trademark has made a comeback, assaulting the market with a triple-barreled distribution strategy. Rexall products are now sold through retail stores, mail order, and network marketing. The company's MLM subsidiary, Rexall Showcase International, was launched in 1990 and now has 25,000 distributors. Analysts Raymond James & Associates—which co-underwrote Rexall's IPO—estimate that given a continueing bull market, Rexall's stock should increase as much as 40 percent in the near term, largely thanks to its use of MLM distribution.

Find the Hidden Relationships

While it's true that sophisticated Wave-Three CEOs are far less shy than their predecessors about raising money through capital markets, it would nevertheless be premature to expect a rash of public offerings from MLM companies. Network marketers have traditionally avoided the stock market. With low overhead and heavy cash flow, successful MLM companies can usually afford to keep their stock all in the family. Even after 33 years, Amway (worth $4.5 billion) remains a closely-held corporation.

The real impact of Wave Three on the stock market will be felt indirectly, by a whole skein of interconnected customers, suppliers, partners, and parent companies whose relation to network marketing is not always clear to the casual observer. Just as Applied Electronics increased its stock price tenfold through its ownership of Quorum, many corporations in the coming years will boost their sales through permanent or temporary alliances with

MLM companies. Keep your eye out for those hidden relationships, and you may spot some amazing opportunities.

SPEED TO MARKET

As the Quorum experience so clearly attests, if there's one thing network marketing can do for a manufacturer, it's to bring a new product to market faster than any other known method. And that can make all the difference in the world.

In *The 22 Immutable Laws of Marketing,* authors Al Ries and Jack Trout state that "It's better to be first than it is to be better." According to this so-called "law of leadership," the market leader in every product category tends to be the one who beats the others to market—even if its competitors come in later with a superior product.

For example, when the painkiller Ibuprofen was invented, Advil, Nuprin, and Medipren entered the market, in that order, with similar products. Guess who's leading today? Advil, with a 51-percent share. How many people remember that Bert Hinkler was the *second* man to fly over the Atlantic? Or that he flew *faster* than Charles Lindbergh and with less waste of fuel? Nobody cares.[1]

For that reason, speed to market is one of the surest indicators of a company's long-term success. And network marketing is one of the most effective tools to achieve it.

The Distribution Freeway

The network-marketing industry is rapidly evolving into a gigantic distribution freeway, with an established infrastructure of trained distributors, high-tech information channels, and even ready-made access to foreign markets.

---

1. The preceding two paragraphs are paraphrased and partly quoted from a review I wrote in *Success* magazine, July/August 1993.

As Amway has demonstrated brilliantly, this distribution freeway can be used by any company—not just the MLM company itself. Amway, for example, moves products and services for MCI, Coca-Cola, Firestone, Chevrolet, and many other leading brand names.

In the future, network-marketing companies will serve more as distribution freeways than as a specialized sales force for a single manufacturer. Astute investors will take note of the rapidly formed virtual alliances that take place along that freeway.

EVANESCENCE: THE MIRACLE OF PERFECT TIMING

The corporate world is abuzz with talk about "virtual corporations," defined by *Business Week* as "a temporary network of companies that come together quickly to exploit fast-changing opportunities. . . . After the business is done, it disbands."

One of the key strengths of a virtual corporation is its *evanescence*. It can appear and disappear in the wink of an eye. Unlike corporate divisions and departments of government, virtual corporations last precisely as long as they're needed—and not a nanosecond longer.

MLM alliances fit this model perfectly. To use network marketing, a company needn't make a permanent commitment.

US Sprint benefited mightily from its alliance with the MLM company Network 2000. With its sales reps hawking US Sprint long-distance service on every street corner in America, the fledgling company quickly siezed a sizeable chunk of AT & T's market share.

But then it came time to digest its gains. US Sprint had reached the limits of its furious growth. Now it needed to focus on customer service and renewal business. The circus atmosphere of its original sales blitz no longer seemed appropriate to the image of an established, growing company which US Sprint wished to convey. To this day, Network 2000 still sells US Sprint. But US Sprint has switched the focus of its marketing efforts to a conventional direct sales force.

It is just such evanescent flashes of MLM growth that provide the most fertile soil for attentive Wave-Three investors.

A POWERFUL SUPPLEMENT

In the priorities of the Wave-Three distributor, the fifth income stream should never rival or replace the real work of network marketing, which is retailing and recruiting. Nevertheless, it provides a powerful supplement to the traditional opportunities offered by network marketing.

Before this century is out, every industry will seek its own unique interface with the distribution freeway. And, for many of those industries, that interface will turn out to be network marketing.

Like the travelling merchants of ancient times, Wave-Three distributors will move with ease between the warring power blocs of the wealthy and the mighty. More than any other sector of society, they will wield privileged access to the pulsing arteries of goods and information by which 21st-century industry will thrive. And, from their eagle's eyries, the Wave-Three distributors will spot before anyone else those fleeting alliances that signal opportunity, those virtual corporations that congeal and dissemble in the blink of an eye amid the bubbling protoplasm of the economy.

Thus, the age-old quest for personal power comes full circle—the lowly peddler has become the master investor, determining the fate of industries behind the scenes. And, while working his or her humble business as diligently as ever, the network marketer grows quietly prosperous from the most powerful residual of all—the fifth income stream.

Chapter 10

WAVE FOUR AND BEYOND

I magine it's the year 2010 A.D.

You do all your shopping directly from the telescreen. Every product or service you could ever imagine can be ordered electronically and delivered to your door in 24 hours.

Sound convenient? Don't be too sure!

Turn on your telescreen and move your cursor to the "grocery" icon. Suddenly, you're strolling through a supermarket as vast as the Hanging Gardens of Babylon. Aisles of products stretch to every horizon. From each shelf, animated images of genetically-engineered "groceries" dance, cavort, and call you by name.

A sealed package of irradiated hydroponic beans flashes strobe lights into your retina, while a strange, hypnotic voice whispers "Buy me, buy me," in perfect synchronization to your brain's theta-wave frequency. As you reach out involuntarily to grab the product, your trance is suddenly shattered by other packages nearby that bark, scream, or simulate automatic gunfire, air raid sirens, or fingernails scraping along a blackboard.

"Don't listen to him!" they cry. "Buy me instead!"

Over in the produce section, a crate of overgrown cucumbers cracks Jimmy Durante-style one-liners: "I'm not your nose! I'm a genetically altered cucumber! Hot-cha-

cha-cha-cha!" You blush as you pass a shelf of ripe toma-
toes, undulating obscenely and whispering explicit sexual
come-ons into your ear.

Each product has its own unique style. But they're all
after the same prize. They want you to click your cursor
over them. Be careful! The moment you click, you'll be
under their control. Your screen will explode into a phan-
tasmagoria of interactive programs, focusing on that particular product. Prompts for "customer testimonials,"
"complaint and litigation history," "nutritional information"—even "celebrity endorsements"—will parade across
your field of vision in dazzling color, accompanied by flash-
ing lights and rhythmic white noise designed to neutralize
your psychological resistance.

In short, shopping in the year 2010 will be a nightmare.

THE WAVE-THREE SOLUTION

This fantasy scenario may be a slight exaggeration. But not
much of one. For all its convenience, electronic marketing
will prove a disturbing and jarring experience for most people. Only Wave Three, the return of the human element, will
offer relief from the shopping horrors of the future.

Person-to-person selling has been used for thousands
of years, and network marketing for at least 50 years. But
there has never been a more desperate need for them than
today.

The reason is *information overload.*

There was a time when people thought computers
would simplify our lives. Managers dreamed of "paperless
offices." Employees dreamed of goofing off all day while
"smart systems" did their work for them. Dream on! Everyone knows today that computers only add complexity,
paper, confusion, and *work* to any office.

So it is with the information superhighway. Already, people are overwhelmed by the sheer volume of raw data that assails them every day. As interactive television replaces the shopping mall, information overload will reach a crisis point. People will feel trapped in a consumer cyberspace whose weirdness will awe, anger, and intimidate the most intrepid shopper.

Only massive human intervention will ease the crisis.

Think what a relief it is to finally get a real, live person on the phone, after you've spent 30 minutes arguing with a voice-mail system about that mistake on your credit-card bill. In the 21st century, network marketers will be the real people who will guide you safely through the datastream jungle.

"We're on the threshold of a new communications era," says Wayne McIlvaine, former marketing director for McCann-Erickson advertising agency. Some of the world's largest corporations—including General Foods, Campbell's Soup, Phillip Morris, and Nabisco—go to McIlvaine to learn what the future holds for their industries. And, to company after company, McIlvaine advises . . . network marketing!

"Network marketing is the wave of the future," he says. "Major corporations are already having to embrace the fact that they will no longer have four TV networks to advertise on, but a hundred. They're looking at the fact that they can buy six hours a day of television time to do educational selling, instead of 30-to-60-seconds. . . . Therein lies the great opportunity for network marketing. Because it may be difficult for people to find out how to access all this information without help from a network marketer."

THE HUMAN DIFFERENCE

Let's go back to our fantasy of life in the year 2010.

You rely on network marketers every day. Without them, life would be terrifying. Your network-marketing friends always seem to have an inside line on the best buys. You trust their opinions because you know them personally and see them using the products. Most important of all, following their advice saves you from having to venture into the datastream jungle yourself!

Take your next-door neighbor. She sells cars. She guides you through the spaghetti-like mass of digitized infomercials, suggesting which cars you should check out from all the thousands of available models, then directs your attention to those specific prompts that focus on key selling points of the car. If you like one particular car, she'll contact the local dealer and show up at your doorstep in a demo model of the newest Mexican or Indonesian import.

What's really amazing about your next-door neighbor is that she doesn't use the kinds of high-pressure sales manipulation that assault you in the datastream jungle. She doesn't flash strobe lights in your face. She doesn't use neurolinguistic programming. She doesn't "mirror" your gestures, stare at your solar plexus to assess your breathing style, nor study your eyeball movements to determine whether you're a visual or kinesthetic personality type. In fact, she makes no attempt whatever to brainwash you, hypnotize you, or otherwise program you. All she does is listen to your problems, suggest solutions, and let you decide.

In the end, you're so grateful for being treated like a human being that you'd never dream of buying a car from anyone else.

THE LIMITS OF CONTROL

A hundred years ago, when the Machine Age was just beginning, people feared that the machine would someday enslave mankind. The 1920s science fiction movie *Metropolis* envisioned a mechanized city of the future peopled with faceless, lifeless automatons milling about like ants. That nightmare vision almost came to pass. Managers in the '20s imposed "efficiency" training on employees, binding workers to assembly-lines, where the machine set the pace and the worker just had to keep up. Architects designed buildings in the form of giant glass and steel boxes whose windows could not be opened—structures more suitable for robot habitation than human.

At the root of Machine-Age thinking was the idea that people could be controlled just like machines. We see the last vestiges of this delusion in the teachings of management guru W. Edwards Deming, who urged managers to measure statistically every detail of a work team's performance. We also see it in the spread of new software that actually "spies" on computer users and reports to their managers whenever they slack off in their work effort.

But that's all coming to an end. Experts predict that, in the 21st century, machine-like rationality will play second fiddle to the spiritual, moral, and social bonds between men and women in the workplace.

"Firms . . . have begun to reach the limits of rationality as a strategy for controlling workers," writes management professor Nicole Woolsey Biggart in *Charismatic Capitalism: Direct Selling Organizations in America*. "Workers who feel like cogs . . . in the corporate machinery, display predictable pathologies: alienation, burnout . . . absenteeism, low productivity, even sabotage."

It is network marketing, with its "less rational" way of doing things, that Biggart believes heralds the managerial style of the future. Network marketing returns control to the individual. And it makes the machine serve people, rather than the reverse.

The Hands-Off Revolution

Network marketing is no low-tech business. On the contrary, it relies upon the most advanced technology on the market. But it uses that technology to simplify work, rather than complicate it.

For example, Nu Skin distributors Tom and Terry Hill keep track of a global downline of over 5,000 distributors, using nothing but a telephone and a set of index cards.

People like the Hills can afford to throw away their PCs precisely because their parent company, Nu Skin, is so loaded down with megabytes at the home office. If the Hills want to know who's in their downline, they call a dedicated information line and request an updated, computerized printout. Ditto for the latest figures on sales and commissions. If they wish to send an announcement to their downline, they call another number, say the message into the phone, and then punch a code on their telephone keypad, which transmits that message instantaneously to the voice mailboxes of their distributors—or, if they choose, to just one particular distributor. Similarly, the Hills check into their voice mailbox periodically for messages from their upline, downline, or from the Nu Skin home office.

"When I send out information to a prospect," says Tom Hill, "it's usually in the form of a video or an audio or printed material that the company has already created, and I just take a little Post-It and write a handwritten note to the individual."

WAVE FOUR: A NATION OF NETWORKERS

If things keep going the way they are, network marketing will eventually become so easy that virtually anyone can do it, anywhere, anytime. We will become a nation of networkers—part-time salespeople who make residual income every time they recommend a product to a friend.

Imagine one more time that it's the year 2010. You're the last person in America who refuses to become a network marketer. All your neighbors are doing it. All your friends, relatives, and professional colleagues. But not you. You're still holding out stubbornly.

Even your boss is a network marketer. He works out of his home in the woods of northern California, while you live in Telluride, CO. But the two of you meet by video-conference two or three times a week.

"Have you tried Diet-Gel, Dick?" he'll ask at the end of a meeting. "It's great stuff. I lost 15 pounds last week eating it. It's the same stuff the astronauts ate on the first Mars mission."

"I'm not really looking to lose weight right now," you protest.

"That's okay. Someday you might. I'll remind you from time to time. You don't mind if I just enter my ID number in your Diet-Gel program, do you?"

What that means is the next time you buy Diet-Gel at the interactive supermarket, your boss Harry automatically gets his commission from your purchase—even if it's ten years after this conversation.

"By the way," he adds before signing off, "have you seen that new movie, *Anti-Terror Avengers?* It's great! Warring drug gangs wipe out Manhattan with a suitcase neutron bomb, and then the ATA squad retaliates by declaring martial law and throwing millions of suspects into detention camps all over America."

"Uh, I don't know, Harry. It sounds too much like real life. I moved out here to the Rockies to get away from all that."

"Well, in case you change your mind, er uh, do you mind . . ."

"No, Harry, I don't mind. You have my permission to tag that movie with your ID number. No problem."

And so life goes. You have so many thousands of different peoples' ID numbers tagging different products and services on your home shopping programs that most of the time you have no idea who makes money on what. You tell yourself over and over that you don't care. But you're beginning to feel left out.

It's hard to forget that every man, woman, and child you know gets a computerized commission check every month from the hundreds of goods and services they're touting to all their friends and neighbors. Moreover, they get to purchase all those same goods and services themselves at a wholesale discount, which can run as high as 50 percent.

You're beginning to suspect that you're the last person in America who pays full retail price for anything!

"These network-marketing companies," grumps the elderly host of your favorite telescreen talk show, a woman who used to be a prominent news anchor back in the '80s and '90s, "they don't pay you a cent unless you actually sell something! I've been warning people against network marketing for 20 years. How can people still keep falling for it?"

"Atta-girl!" you cry from your overstuffed chair. "You tell 'em! We'll never give in. We'll never be network marketers. *Never!*"

But deep down inside, you know it's only a matter of time . . .

It's Coming

This futuristic scenario is closer than you may think.

As in many other respects, Nu Skin has pioneered the technology of Wave-Three network marketing. Its Retail Advantage program has been in place since 1991. Other companies, like Reliv, have followed with similar programs. Such dropshipping programs allow customers to pick out products from a catalog and order them through a toll-free number. The operator will ask for the distributor reference number printed on the catalog. This number is unique to the distributor who gave the catalog to the customer. It ensures that the distributor will get his or her commission from the order. Without a distributor's reference number, the operator won't place the order.

"Within hours after that order's input," says Tom Hill of Nu Skin, "it's on a truck heading to the airport. So my only job is to pick up the phone and call people and shake their hands."

Hill may not even know the order was placed until the end of the month when he gets a printout and a commission check for it.

McIlvaine praises such dropshipping programs as an important step on the road to Wave Three.

"All of a sudden, there's a different attitude," he says. "Distributors are sensing 'I don't have to have a home party, I don't have to go door to door to sell. I can just communicate and order.'"

Nu Skin distributors already look forward to more advanced programs now in development.

"When interactive TV comes on line," says Hill, "you'll hand a customer a catalog on a laserdisc, and the customer plugs that disc into their disc player and sees someone talking about the products, explaining them. If they want to buy something, they just use their zapper. And embedded on that disc will be our own unique ID number, so that we get credit for the sale."

Get in on the Ground Floor

Ten or fifteen years from now, today's media attacks on the network-marketing industry will read like pages from the Salem witch trials. Network marketing will be so pervasive in society, it won't even qualify any longer as a separate and distinct industry. It will be a standard tool used by every industry.

Those with foresight will get in now, on the ground floor. Now is the time to master the fundamentals. Now is the time to build your network. Be prepared. For very soon, your friends, relatives, and colleagues will be turning to you en masse, begging you to guide them through the datastream jungle of the 21st century.

Chapter 11

It's More than Money

"**A**ccording to the American Medical Association," says John Fogg, editor of *Upline,* "more fatal heart attacks occur at 9 A.M., Monday morning than at any other time in the week. More first-time heart attacks occur between 8 A.M. and 10 A.M. on Monday mornings, too. And, according to the National Institute of Health, more strokes—the number three cause of death in America—also occur between 8 and 9 in the morning.

"The obvious conclusion?" asks Fogg. "People would rather die than go back to work."

Only half-jokingly, Fogg suggests a new recruiting slogan for network marketers: "Network marketing—the life you save could be your own!"

Peace of Mind Through Network Marketing

In a world where competition grows keener by the day, and the demands on overworked employees ever more cruel, stress in the workplace has become a real threat to life, liberty, and the pursuit of happiness. Network marketing offers real relief.

The vast majority of networkers earn only modest income from their businesses. Yet they gain a treasure more priceless than gold: Peace of mind. Even part-time networkers gain greater control over their lives, since, from the moment they receive their first commission check, their livelihood no longer depends solely upon one job and one boss.

It's Not About Money

Contrary to popular belief, surveys indicate that most network marketers are not interested in getting rich. MLM newsletter *MarketWave* polled nearly 1,000 network marketers, asking, "What income level do you realistically hope to achieve in network marketing?"

The answers were shocking.

"Over 86 percent claimed they would have been satisfied with only an extra $250 per month," says *MarketWave* publisher Leonard Clements, "or with a little extra time flexibility, say, replacing their current family income, but having one person in the family work 20 *flexible* hours to achieve it, rather than two people working 40 *fixed* hours a week."

In other words, most people in network marketing have no expectation or pressing desire to get rich. All they want is a little extra money, and a little extra time.

Beverly Hills International distributor Marjorie Musselman went through many ups and downs in her network-marketing career, changing companies several times over the years. But, despite the rocky road, Musselman achieved her objectives. After her husband was laid off, her commission checks put food on the table and helped her husband start his own insurance company after he had gotten laid off from his job. For Musselman, a few hundred extra dollars a month proved her salvation. And the occasional checks that came in for $1,600, $2,000, or more were received in the Musselman house like manna from heaven.

"When I got a check for $2,800," she declares, "for me, that was like getting a million dollars!"

THE INTANGIBLES: MORE IMPORTANT THAN GETTING RICH

Clearly, the vast majority of networkers enter the business for reasons much less tangible than money. These reasons—the *intangibles*, we might call them—will loom far larger in importance as Wave Three gains ground in the industry.

On the horizon looms a profound shift in the culture of network marketing. Some of the changes have already started. In the sales pitches of today's sophisticated networker, phrases like "time flexibility" and "substantial part-time income" have taken the place of fallacious promises of overnight wealth and startling, exponential arithmetic scrawled on the backs of envelopes and restaurant napkins.

The Wave-Three culture takes little notice of the occasional MLM millionaire. Its heroes are ordinary, hardworking folk. Wave-Three networkers no longer join MLM companies in the distant hope of attaining millions. They join to find a style of living that satisfies their hunger for personal liberty and fulfillment.

Noble Deeds

Freed from drudgery by new systems and technology, Wave-Three networkers can focus their energies on nobler pursuits. A machine can be programmed to make money. A computer can run a business. But only a human being is capable of true generosity. Only a man or woman can enjoy the profound satisfaction that comes from bettering the world. It is in the realm of good deeds that the Wave-Three revolution makes its finest and clearest mark.

Residual Impact

Through their network-marketing businesses, distributors achieve something far more powerful than "residual income." They achieve what John Fogg calls "residual impact."

"When you sit on top of an organization of 50,000 people," says Fogg, "and you know that 50,000 men and women out there are more financially able, secure, and free, and that their lives have changed because of you, that's residual impact. Once you're at that point, you can never shake the feeling. You can never retire. People at that level are addicted like a drug to changing the lives of others for the better. You never get off it, never, never, never!"

Residual impact gives you more than just gushy feelings. More than in most other businesses, generosity in MLM often translates directly into cold, hard cash.

For example, after donating $150,000 to the United Way in Reno, Nu Skin superstar Mark Yarnell was voted "Philanthropist of the Year" for northern Nevada. At the meeting where he received his plaque, a successful banker approached Yarnell and joined his downline.

"In 1992 alone, her efforts could easily net me more than the entire $150,000 I donated to the United Way," says Yarnell.

THE RELIGION OF THE NEXT MILLENNIUM?

"Network marketing may be the religion of the next millennium," declares John Fogg.

Fogg points out that the qualities of a great sponsor are similar to those that every great religion tries to foster in its acolytes: integrity, honor, compassion, charity. The ideal network-marketing company should be a brotherhood of honest and hardworking folk, whose lives center not around a corporate rat race but around friendship, service, and communion with one another—not unlike the ideal *church!*

"But when the collection basket is passed," quips Fogg, "instead of you dropping money *in,* money drops *out* into your lap."

Christian Charity

For Mark Yarnell, network marketing proved far more elevating than his Christian ministry. As the pastor of a country church, Yarnell found he spent more time meditating on petty politics than on the grace of God.

"I was always trying to negotiate arguments between the ladies' auxiliary who wanted to do a bakesale and the teenagers who wanted to do a carwash on the same day."

As related earlier, Yarnell was "rescued" after ten years by financial disaster, which forced him to seek—and eventually find—his fortune in network marketing. In the process, Yarnell found something he never expected—spiritual fulfillment.

"When I was in seminary, studying for the ministry," says Yarnell, "I learned five magic words: 'I will pray with you.' Now I've got five new words: 'How much do you need?' That's the big difference between being a minister and being a successful network marketer."

Yarnell has found his greatest satisfaction in giving to the needy. After seeing a newscast about a crippled police officer whose department had only managed to raise half the money to buy him an electric wheelchair, Yarnell promptly wrote out a check to cover the rest.

"Back when I was a preacher," says Yarnell, "I would have watched that broadcast and I would have thought, geez, I hope he gets the money. But now it means nothing to me to write a check for $1,800 to help somebody. I can make a difference now."

In the course of his charitable work, Yarnell has written checks for considerably more than $1,800. He once made a record contribution to the United Way of $150,000. And when Patricia McCune, a close friend of then-Senator Al Gore, asked the Yarnells for help in founding the International Green Cross, the Yarnells helped pay her way to the environmental summit in Rio de Janeiro to meet with Mikhail Gorbachev.

"We had the money and time to help fund that project, which now has a thousand new chapters in 75 countries," writes his wife, René Reid Yarnell in *Should You Quit Before You're Fired?*

The urge to preach still strikes Yarnell at times. But now, when he appears as a guest preacher in Christian congregations around the world, Yarnell does it for love, not sustenance.

Doing Well by Doing Good

You don't need a downline 50,000 strong to have residual impact. Nor do you need a six-figure checking account. Even the most ordinary network marketer can have extraordinary impact upon other people—and get paid for it!

Doris Wood once recruited a woman who, for incurable medical reasons, was grossly overweight. The woman was pathologically shy, depressed, filled with shame and anxiety over her physical appearance.

Had she met this woman in normal life, Wood could have done nothing for her. Nor would she have had any reason to try. But Wood was a network marketer. She taught the woman the same lessons she taught all her other recruits—how to sell, sponsor, and train others to sell, sponsor and train. Those simple lessons worked a miracle in the woman's life.

"She started to come out of her shell," Wood remembers. "She got over her defeatist attitude."

The woman never struck it rich. She never went full-time. She simply became one of those millions of happy networkers who manage to supplement their incomes with a few hundred extra dollars a month. But for her, that small achievement opened doors to a new world. With her new-found confidence, the woman decided to pursue her dream of becoming a singer.

"She went on to become one of the top-notch singers in local area clubs," says Wood, who is now president of the Multilevel Marketing International Association (MLMIA) in Irvine, CA. "She sang at all our banquets and award functions. She was *good*. And she earned a considerable amount of money as a nightclub singer.

"When you take somebody like that who couldn't even get a job," Wood concludes, "and you give them the opportunity and help them reach their potential, that's a thrill that has to be experienced to be understood."

LIBERTY AS A GOAL

When Thomas Jefferson asserted the right of all Americans to "life, liberty, and the pursuit of happiness," he had in mind a nation of farmers, each presiding like a king over his private portion of the earth. For Jefferson, land was a key measure of American freedom.

Today, few Americans own land. And, in the 21st century, even fewer will have that opportunity. Our freedom will therefore be measured no longer by our control over physical property, but by the degree of control we exercise over our own *time*.

"Time will be one of the biggest issues and one of the most valued assets in the coming years," says Life Extension International distributor Jerry Rubin.

Network marketing is one of the few known methods by which the masses can gain control over their daily schedules.

The Flextime Revolution

The business world has been buzzing for years over *flex-time*—the practice of letting employees work on a flexible schedule. This is done through such methods as "job-sharing," allowing employees to work at home, or giving them "compressed work weeks," in which they complete their weekly obligations at an accelerated pace. Many companies have experimented with flextime. But don't get your hopes up. Corporate America is not likely to become a worker's paradise anytime soon. Indeed, the backlash against flextime—sometimes euphemized as "family-friendly policies"—has already started.

"Many companies say they can ill afford family-oriented programs in an era of heightened global competition," says the June 28, 1993, issue of *Business Week*. "For small businesses, especially, family-friendly policies can breed resentment among the workers who have to pick up the slack. And for every company that embraces a family-friendly working environment, there are others that merely say they do."

The only real flextime is that which you create for yourself, through self-employment and residual income.

"Network marketing doesn't necessarily give you more time," says Terry Hill of Nu Skin, "but it gives you time *flexibility*. If you miss a meeting, you're not going to lose your job, or lose your check for that month. You can put other things first when you have to, and your business will still function."

RETURN OF THE FAMILY

Hill points to the flextime of network marketing as the glue that holds her family together.

"It's very difficult to be married today," she opines. "Especially if you both have careers. The husband's going one way, the wife's going another. You spend more time with other people than you do with your family."

Network marketing provided the Hills with a way out. Both quit their jobs and worked together on their Nu Skin business. After building their downline for two years, they took off an entire year to get to know their children and one another better. Now they're both back at work. But when the children return from school each day, they find both parents at home.

"We may be busy on the phone," says Hill, "we may have somebody over at the house talking about the business, but we're here. It makes a big difference. So many of our daughters' friends come home to empty houses. Or the younger ones go to a daycare."

Like the pioneer families of old, the Hills work together toward a common goal, sharing their daily dreams and struggles. Whatever they achieve, they achieve in unison.

"There's nothing that will bring you closer," says Hill, "than making sacrifices together and being dedicated to the same goal. It's like going on a journey together. Your children are involved. They're using the products. They see your work effort. They see you setting goals and see how you go about accomplishing them.

"The big difference between us and other people that are trapped in traditional business," Hill concludes, "is that we have a vehicle that allows us to be a family together. We really owe everything about our lives to this business. It's given us a way to live that we wouldn't normally have."

A New Extended Family: The Tribe

In stripping man of his tribal heritage, modern society has left a gaping wound. Telecommunications, jet transport, and global government may soon dissolve what's left of our

national borders, while nursing homes and eugenics finish
off the extended family, but people still crave the kinship
and belonging that came with nightly chants around the
campfire.

In a world growing stranger and lonelier by the
minute, many find in network marketing a sense of community that can only be called *tribal*.

"It fills a gap in the social life of our society," says Doris
Wood. "People can go to opportunity meetings and stand
and give a testimonial, and be welcomed with open arms
because they're part of that group. In this society, where
people are so transient and we don't have great aunts and
uncles and brothers and sisters around, network marketing almost takes the place of the extended family."

Global Tribes

The tribal metaphor is perhaps more apt than it first appears. In his influential book, *Tribes: How Race, Religion
and Identity Determine Success in the New Global Economy,* author Joel Kotkin claims that tribalism is making a
comeback. He argues that the intimate personal networks
arising from ethnic, family, and religious ties may soon replace the nation–state as the most formidable force on
earth. Kotkin points to groups like the Mormons, the Chinese, and the Jains (a close-knit sect of Indian mystics who
dominate global diamond markets) as examples of "global
tribes" whose common faith and social bonds reinforce
their effectiveness as transnational power blocs.

Although Kotkin doesn't say so, network-marketing
downlines often exhibit the same proclivities for worldwide
organization, rapid global response, and close personal ties
as do more familiar tribes like the Chinese or the Hasidim.
If Kotkin's vision comes to pass, MLM companies may
someday resemble transnational states, whose treasuries
rival those of powerful nations, and whose "citizens" work

in unison on every continent of the earth, united only by computer network and a common tribal vision.

Gods and Heroes

Every tribe, of course, has its own sense of purpose, its tales of gods and heroes that spell out the unique mission of the race. From the story of Isis and Osiris, the Egyptians derived their perennial fascination with life after death. In the midnight ride of Paul Revere, we Americans remember the spirit of rebellion that gave rise to our nation.

In this respect, the Wave-Three company will look far more like a tribe than a sales organization. Its mission will be expressed not in dollars and cents, but in terms of the loftiest ideals.

A REVOLUTIONARY MOVEMENT

"Amway is more than a company," Amway co-founder Richard DeVos told *Forbes*. "It's a movement."

Amway has long understood the power of tribal vision in building a network-marketing business. Its mass rallies open to the stirring strains of the *Rocky* theme song or *Chariots of Fire*. They feature sermons on family life and personal integrity, delivered in meeting halls festooned with stars and stripes. No Amway distributor can ever forget that his or her company stands for something far deeper than a business opportunity. It stands for the American Way.

In his book *Compassionate Capitalism,* Richard DeVos describes his company's revolutionary mission, starting from its founding in 1959. When DeVos and Jay Van Andel founded Amway, Fidel Castro was enjoying sympathetic coverage in the American press. Some Americans were beginning to suspect that Russia would indeed "bury" America, as Khrushchev later threatened. And many had already resigned themselves to the prospect of a socialist future.

"In those days," writes DeVos, "socialism was regarded as the world's great economic hope. Free enterprise was dead. At least that's what Jay and I were told . . . Russia and China were . . . bound to triumph . . . 'This is no time to go into business for yourself,' some people warned us. 'Those days have passed forever . . . Capitalism has failed and it will fail again. Socialism is our only hope.'"

Needless to say, DeVos and Van Andel gave this advice the response it deserved. They ignored it. Today, Amway preaches its gospel of free enterprise in 60 countries, through more than 2 million distributors. Sales have doubled in the last three years, reaching $4.5 billion for fiscal 1993.

In *Compassionate Capitalism,* DeVos tells of a Mexican peasant woman who told him in halting English that the simple dress she wore was the first she'd been able to buy in her life—thanks to her involvement with Amway. He relates how a young East German father thanked DeVos with tears in his eyes for giving him a fresh start as an Amway distributor after the fall of the Berlin Wall. An embittered African-American who had refused all his life to pledge allegiance to the flag now salutes Old Glory, teary-eyed, at Amway conventions, having found at last a community that judges him on merit alone—the community of entrepreneurs and business owners, as exemplified by Amway, whose very name is derived from the "American Way."[1]

Critics of Amway often mock its distributors for their fanatical allegiance to the cause. Their starry-eyed devotion is sometimes attributed to brainwashing. But if Amway's dis-

---

1. This paragraph is paraphrased and partly quoted from a review of *Compassionate Capitalism,* which I wrote in the June 1993 issue of *Success.*

tributors suffer from impaired judgment, the intoxicant seems to be idealism. Amway's leaders discovered early that most people will hesitate to give their last ounce of strength in pursuit of their own self-interest. But for a cause larger than themselves, they will forfeit their very lives.

DO IT AGAIN!

In 1968, radical leader Jerry Rubin wrote and published a handbook of youthful rebellion called *Do It!* The book became a national bestseller.

"I went to every college campus, with my painted face and my headband, screaming 'Do it!'" says Rubin. "I was telling people you can be free, you can be any way you want to be. We don't have to fit into the corporate mold. We don't have to look the way we're supposed to look. We don't have to be mass-produced people."

Today, as a frontline distributor for Life Extension International, Rubin is once again telling people to "Do it!" When he runs ads in national newspapers, Rubin's phone rings off the hook with disillusioned professionals seeking an alternate income.

"I ask them, 'Is your boss there?'" says Rubin. "'You mean he's sitting right across from you? Stand up and tell your boss, "Hey, you're fired."' They all laugh when I say that."

In network marketing, the '60s spirit of rebellion has come face to face with the American heartland—and melded with it! Like the patriots of 1776, network marketers crave liberty above life itself. But like the hippies of 1967, they pursue that freedom through lifestyle, rather than force of arms. For many networkers, the necktie remains as much a symbol of servitude as it was for the Yippies!

"When I go prospecting, I wear khaki pants and a polo shirt and occasionally a sport coat but never a tie," says

Mark Yarnell. "I want to portray the image of freedom. I want them to understand that I can wear anything I want. I can do anything I want. I don't have to wear a tie like they do."

The "Greening" of America

Today, when so many bitter issues divide our nation, network marketing provides one of the few ties that binds. In his vision of a self-employed America, erstwhile radical Jerry Rubin has found common cause with flag-wavers like DeVos and Van Andel.

Together, they and their constituencies are rebuilding America. And however that new America finally shapes up, it's bound to look a whole lot more like the nation our Founding Fathers envisioned than the bureaucratic Corporate America that Carl Rehnborg challenged when he started Nutrilite all those decades ago.

Appendix

COMPENSATION PLANS—
THE INSIDE STORY

"Infinite depth!"
 "75 percent payout!"
 "Massive spillover potential!"
 "More money upfront!"
 Which do you choose? Whom do you believe? What does it all mean? Choosing a compensation plan can be a daunting exercise. The comp plan, or marketing plan, is the method by which a network marketing company divides commissions among its distributors. The comp plan largely determines how much money you'll make, and how quickly, for a given amount of work. *When choosing a company, pay close attention to the comp plan.*

Unfortunately, even long-time MLM veterans seldom know what to look for in a comp plan. No area of network marketing is more clouded with mystery, more fraught with myth.

"Comp plan design is without a doubt the most perception-oriented aspect of the business," says *MarketWave* publisher Leonard Clements. "There are tons of ways to make a plan appear more lucrative on paper but in reality have it pay no more than any other plan."

The following guidelines for analyzing a compensation plan draw from the wisdom of noted experts Leonard Clements, Corey Augenstein, Dr. Srikumar Rao, and others.

SEVEN CRITERIA FOR CHOOSING A COMP PLAN

1. *Simplicity.* The easier a plan is to explain, the easier it is to persuade new recruits to sign up. When people can't figure out how their commissions are calculated, they tend to suspect they're getting a snow job. And often they're right. Beware of plans that seem unnecessarily confusing and complicated.

2. *Potential Size of Organization.* Two factors affect the potential size of your organization—width and depth. Make sure you know exactly what limits your comp plan places on the width and depth of your organization. Only matrix plans place limits on width, which is the number of people you are allowed to place in your frontline. But all comp plans limit your depth to a certain number of levels. Depth can be tricky. For reasons explained below, a six-level stairstep/breakaway plan might allow you to draw commissions from twice as many levels as a six-step unilevel plan. So even though both are described as six-level plans, one actually has more depth than the other.

3. *Front end or back end?* Some plans stack their higher commissions onto the "backend"—meaning *after* you break away or build down to your lower levels. Such a plan may offer one percent commission on level one, but 20 percent on level six. Such "back-end" plans are far more lucrative in the long run because the geometric growth of your downline will place huge numbers of people on the lower levels, where your commissions are biggest. But that

only works for ambitious, energetic, and persistent distributors who work long and hard to build an organization deep enough to access those big commissions.

Half-hearted, part-time networkers may never build an organization deeper than one or two levels, and so those big numbers on the back end are of no use to them. Generally, the choice boils down to this: Back end means hard work, delayed gratification, and bigger long-term rewards; front end means more money upfront, with less effort, but smaller long-term earning potential. The choice is yours.

4. ***Profit Potential.*** To estimate the profit potential of a comp plan, MLM trainer Dennis Windsor recommends the following method. First, look at the wholesale discount the company gives you for your product purchases. This discount will vary according to your achievement level in the company. An entry-level distributor might get a 25 percent discount while a qualified executive might be entitled to a 45 percent discount or more. As in any retail business, the *spread* or difference between your wholesale price and the price at which you sell the product to customers represents your retail profit. In analyzing a plan, Windsor recommends that you express this retail profit as a sliding scale, representing the range of profit you would enjoy from entry level to the top achievement level in the company. Thus you might say that retail profit ranges from 25 to 45 percent in a particular company. That is the first criterion in calculating your profit potential.

Next, calculate your wholesale profit. This is the profit you make from selling product at wholesale to your downline. Your wholesale customers will be at lower achievement levels than you and will thus be entitled to correspondingly lesser dis-

counts. Let's say, for instance, that you get a 45 percent wholesale discount as a Three-Star Executive,
and that Two-Star Executives in your company only
get a 35-percent discount. Your spread in any sale to
a Two-Star Executive is therefore 10 percent. That's
your wholesale profit. Calculate the range of wholesale profits you would realize by selling to distributors at each achievement level available in your
company. You might say that the wholesale profit
ranges from 10 to 35 percent. That is the second criterion in calculating your profit potential.

In a stairstep/breakaway plan, there is a third
criterion—the percentage of overrides or royalties
from your breakaway legs. That will be a fixed percentage of commission on the total sales of each
breakaway leg. That percentage is the third and
final criterion in calculating your profit potential.

This method will yield only a rough estimate of
your potential earnings, but it gives you a clear set of
figures by which you can compare one plan to another.

5. **Qualifications.** Find out the minimum personal
volume requirement for the plan you're analyzing.
That's the amount of product you must purchase
each month at wholesale in order to qualify as an
active distributor. Also find out how much product
you must purchase each month to qualify for each
achievement level. If the volume requirements are
too high, you could end up stockpiling more product than you can possibly sell. If they are too low,
your downline may have little motivation to sell
anything at all since they will only have to buy
enough each month for their personal consump-
tion. It's up to you to decide what volume requirements are realistic and appropriate for your needs.

6. **Fine Print.** Many comp plans contain fine print—
important stipulations that are seldom mentioned

to prospects and that are often excluded from recruiting videos and literature—but which nevertheless have a major impact on your business.

Always make a point of finding out what the penalties are for failing to meet your monthly quotas. Some plans will give you a grace period of several months in which to get your sales volume back up to par before busting you down to the next lowest achievement level. Other plans will demote you the first month you miss your quota. A few plans will not only demote you immediately but will demote you back down to entry level, no matter how high your current achievement level. There's nothing wrong with tough penalties. If you wish to work a tough plan, that's your choice. But find out what you're getting into before you sign on the dotted line.

Another important question to ask is how the plan calculates your monthly quotas. Does all the sales volume of your organization count toward your quota? Or only some of it? Many companies only count "unencumbered" volume, that is, sales volume from people in your personal group but not from your breakaway legs. That can make a big difference! Other companies calculate your monthly quotas in terms of "bonus volume" rather than actual sales volume. The bonus volume is always less than the sales volume. You might have sold $1,000 worth of goods in a given month, but the company only considers that you moved $700 worth of bonus volume.

Always find out whether the company has a roll-up feature. That means that if you recruit a "big fish"—a top achiever—into your downline, and he out-performs you in a given month, your prize catch may roll up above you in the company hierarchy. You lose your big fish and his entire organization! Roll-up is an advantageous feature for upline leaders who want to promote the best and brightest distributors into their frontlines. But if you're a low or moderate achiever in a "roll-up" company, the only way to keep a big fish in your organization is to purchase enough product every month to stay in your big fish's achievement level. Again, there's nothing wrong with roll-up. If your big fish is bringing in $15,000 per month for you and you just have to pay $3,000 per month to stay in his achievement level, you're still making out like a bandit. But you don't want to be taken by surprise. Always ask if a company has roll-up.

These are just a few of the more common types of fine print that lie hidden between the lines of many comp plans. In general, probe for any stipulations that tend to reduce your commissions, raise your qualifications, or disqualify portions of your sales volume.

7. *Type of plan.* You should understand the pros and cons of each type of plan and choose the one that suits your needs. Below are detailed discussions of the three major types of comp plan—Stairstep/Breakaway, Matrix, and Unilevel. Although you'll hear many more names for different comp plans, all fall into one of these three categories. The Binary plan, for example, is a form of Matrix, and the Australian plan is a variety of Unilevel.

THE STAIRSTEP/BREAKAWAY PLAN

Description. In a stairstep/breakaway plan, you succeed by ascending a staircase of achievement levels. At each step in your ascent, you are awarded a different honorific title (such as "Gold Executive" or "Three-Star Executive") and permitted to buy product from the company at a correspondingly deeper discount. The more product you buy from the company each month, the higher you ascend up the ladder, and the higher your commission.

As you ascend, so do the people in your downline. As soon as your downline distributors ascend to the point where they are moving a certain volume per month, they "break away" from your personal group. You no longer receive a direct commission on product sold to them or to their downline. However, you continue to collect a royalty or override—a small commission—on the total group volume of your breakaways and their downlines.

Advantages of the Stairstep/Breakaway

Unlimited earning potential. Of all comp plans, the stairstep/breakaway provides the best opportunity for people to make it big. That's because the breakaway feature allows you to build a larger organization and to draw commissions from a greater number of levels than is possible with other types of plans.

Deeper pay range. Let's say your plan pays out commissions only down to the sixth level. In a unilevel or matrix, that would mean you are forbidden to draw income from your seventh level or lower. But in a stairstep/breakaway, a distributor on your sixth level can break away, after which you collect an override or commission on that distributor's group volume. If that distributor has a six-level organization, that means you're drawing commission from sales occurring on your 12th level! Some breakaway plans let you draw income from as deep as 20 levels down—a depth unattainable in other types of plans.

Bigger downline. The stairstep/breakaway offers unlimited width. You can recruit as many people as you like into your frontline, and they, in turn, can recruit as many

as they like. The depth may be limited to six levels or so.
But you can go as wide as you like, building a huge downline, potentially tens of thousands strong.

Company stability. Companies with stairstep/break-
away plans tend to have a higher survival rate than others, perhaps due to higher corporate profits. Most of the
larger, established companies, such as Amway, Shaklee,
Nu Skin, Quorum, and others, use the stairstep/break-
away. Indeed, Leonard Clements of *MarketWave* states
that 86 percent of all MLM companies seven years old or
older use the stairstep/breakaway.

Disadvantages

Delayed gratification.   Stairstep/breakaway plans tend
to be the hardest to work. Most of the money comes from
the "back end"—from the deeper levels that only become
available to you after you've had a number of breakaways.
That means you have to work long, hard, and successfully
before you start seeing any significant money. Delayed
gratification is the motto of stairstep/breakaways.

High monthly quotas.   Most stairstep/breakaways require that you meet high monthly volume quotas each
month in order to qualify for the best positions or achievement levels. And every time one of your legs breaks away,
the sales volume from that leg is disqualified from being
counted toward your monthly quota. You have to make it
up by recruiting more people. The result is that distributors in stairstep/breakaway plans are under constant pressure to sell product and recruit more people.

Complexity.   Stairstep/breakaway plans tend to be very
complex and difficult to explain to new recruits.

Topheavy Distribution of Commissions. Some network marketers call the stairstep/breakaway the "Republican" plan, because it tends to channel more money to the
top achievers and to the corporation. This is often per-
ceived as a disadvantage. But is it? "Socialist" plans do indeed distribute commissions more evenly through the
ranks. But they also seem to have a statistically lower survival rate. The problem with socialism, in network marketing as in nations, is that an equal share of the pie isn't
worth much if there's no pie to carve up.

For all the above reasons, stairstep/breakaway plans
work best for serious, dedicated network marketers who
are willing to sacrifice, work hard, and delay their gratification. But for those who stay the course, they offer the
best chance to build a substantial residual income.

THE MATRIX PLAN

Description. Like the unilevel and stairstep/breakaway,
the matrix limits your depth, which is the number of levels
on which you can be paid. But unlike other plans, the matrix also limits your width, or the number of people you can
place on your frontline. A typical matrix would be a 2 x 12,
which means that you can have two people on your frontline and 12 levels in your organization. There are no breakaways in a matrix.

Advantages

Spillover. Any recruits you bring into a matrix over and
above the number allotted for your frontline will "spill over"
into your lower levels. For example, if you have a 2 x 12 matrix and you recruit six people, four of them will spill over
into your second level. Theoretically, this means that a per-

son can just sit in a matrix organization and do nothing, waiting for some high achiever in his upline to build a downline for him through spillover.

Easy to manage. In stairstep/breakaway and unilevel plans, you can theoretically have up to 100 or more people in your frontline, people you are directly responsible for training and sponsoring. In a matrix, you only have to sponsor the two to three people in your frontline.

Simplicity. Matrix plans are very simple to explain to new recruits.

Disadvantages

Lazy downlines. Matrix plans tend to attract people who don't want to work; they want their upline to build an organization for them through spillover.

The Leech Effect. Matrix plans tend to be "socialist" in their distribution of commissions, rewarding top achievers less and non-achievers more. Top achievers get less return on their investment of time and energy because a greater share of commissions is sucked up, leech-like, by downlines full of lazy, spillover junkies.

Limits to Growth. Matrix plans limit the size of your organization. In a 2 x 4 matrix, for example, you can never have more than 120 people in your downline. A stairstep/ breakaway or unilevel plan allows you to have that many people in your frontline alone.

Government Scrutiny. Because of the spillover effect, matrix plans can be "played" almost like a lottery. Their excessive reliance on luck has aroused the ire of government regulators, who tend to scrutinize these plans more than others.

The Unilevel Plan

Description. Like all comp plans, the unilevel has limited depth—that is, a set number of levels on which you are allowed to draw commissions. Like the stairstep/breakaway, it has achievement levels that you attain by maintaining a certain monthly volume. Also like the stairstep/breakaway, the unilevel has unlimited width. You can recruit as many people into your frontline as you like. But the unilevel does not allow breakaways. You might think of the unilevel as a stairstep/breakaway without breakaways.

Advantages

Simplicity. Because it lacks breakaways, the unilevel is very simple to explain to new recruits.

Unlimited Width. As in stairstep/breakaway plans, the unilevel allows you to recruit an unlimited number of people into your frontline.

Spillover. Unilevel plans often stack their highest commission percentages on the third level. For example, the first two levels may pay out one percent each and the third level 50 percent. Distributors will thus put as many new recruits as possible on their third level. Since every distributor's third level corresponds to someone else's first level, that means that each distributor with three or more levels in his or her organization is helping to build someone else's frontline.

Easy qualifications. Because there are no breakaways, and no concept of encumbered and unencumbered volume in a unilevel plan, all the sales volume of your organization counts toward your monthly quotas all the time, no matter what. You don't lose volume every time someone breaks away. You don't have to rush madly each month to make up for volume lost when someone breaks away, as you so often do in stairstep/breakaway plans.

Disadvantages

Limits to growth. Because it lacks breakaways, the unilevel plan only pays out on a small number of levels. Theoretically, you can make up for this by recruiting wide—putting a huge number of people into your frontline. But although unilevel plans place no limits on the number of people you can personally sponsor, there are physical limits to the number you can sponsor effectively. All other factors being equal, a unilevel organization will tend to be smaller than a stairstep/breakaway organization.

Laziness. Because unilevel plans limit growth, they tend to attract a less ambitious breed of distributor, the type more interested in being a wholesale buyer than in building a large downline.

Note: All the advice and insights contained in this appendix were based on interviews and published writings of experts Leonard Clements, Corey Augenstein, Dr. Srikumar Rao, and others. No two of these experts agreed on every point. Any errors of emphasis, fact, or judgment contained herein are the author's sole responsibility.

GLOSSARY OF NETWORK MARKETING TERMS

Achievement Level: A position in a network marketing organization that a distributor obtains usually by purchasing a certain amount of product at wholesale in a given month. The more product you purchase, the higher your position. The higher your position, the deeper your discounts for purchasing product at wholesale. In a stairstep/breakaway plan, achievement levels are also called *stairsteps.*

Back End: The later, more advanced stages that a distributor reaches after progressing through a compensation plan. For example, you might say that a breakaway plan pays more on the back end because you get higher commissions *after* you break away. In other plans, *back end* corresponds to the lower or deeper levels of a comp plan, as when a plan pays 5 percent on the first level, but 20 percent on the third level, thus paying a larger percentage on the back end.

Benefits: Any form of payment or compensation that a distributor derives from working a network marketing business. Can include bonuses, overrides, retail and wholesale commissions, or special perks and premiums.

Breakaway: A distributor who has "broken away" from his sponsor's personal group by meeting certain monthly volume qualifications. Usually, the breakaway's monthly volume no longer counts as part of the monthly group volume of the breakaway's sponsor. However, the sponsor will continue collecting a royalty or override from that breakaway, which is a small percentage of that breakaway's organizational volume.

Breakaway Leg: The entire organization of a breakaway distributor.

Bonus Pool: Money that a network marketing company reserves from its total profits to distribute to a handful of qualifying top achievers as an added incentive.

Bonus Volume: See BV, below.

Buy-Back Policy: A network marketing company's policy regarding refunds on product inventory a distributor has purchased but then fails to sell. All reputable companies will give such refunds, usually for 70–100 percent of wholesale price.

BV (Bonus Volume): The value, usually less than the wholesale price, that a network marketing company assigns to the products its distributors buy at wholesale. Some companies calculate overrides and commissions from bonus volume rather than from wholesale volume. For example, if you sell $100 worth of product at wholesale to your downline and receive a 5 percent commission, that 5 percent will be taken from your BV—which may be calculated at $80—rather than from the full wholesale volume of $100. When you join a company, always ask whether commissions are calculated on the BV, rather than on the wholesale price. Sometimes called point volume (PV) or business volume (BV).

Commission: Retail or wholesale profit that a network marketing distributor earns by selling product to customers or to distributors in his or her downline.

Compression: A feature of some compensation plans that allows a distributor to draw commissions from sales of high achievers who are so deep in the distributor's downline as to fall below his or her ordinary pay range. For example, if you're working a six-level breakaway plan, you are not ordinarily entitled to draw commissions from levels seven or lower. But a plan with compression may count only six levels of high activity (levels on which you have qualified executives or breakaways). Inactive levels, where nobody is selling, don't count. Thus you may "compress" ten or more levels into six "active" levels and draw commissions from a "sixth" level that may actually be ten levels down from you.

Concentration Phase: The second phase of a network marketing company's growth, falling between the ground-floor phase and the momentum phase. The phrase comes from the four-phase system of Professor Charles King.

Depth: The maximum number of levels from which a particular compensation plan allows a distributor to draw commissions. A plan that is six levels deep allows you to draw commissions from only six levels.

Direct Selling: Any type of selling that uses independent representatives working on commission. Network marketing is a type of direct selling, but not the only one. Only those direct selling companies that permit their representatives to recruit other representatives and draw commissions from the sales of their recruits are properly called network marketing companies. *Note:* Some network marketing companies only refer to themselves as "direct sales" companies to conceal the fact that they use an MLM compensation structure.

Distributor: An independent sales representative of a network marketing company.

Downline: All the distributors below you in the chain of recruitment and sponsorship of a given network marketing company—that is, the people recruited by your recruits, and so on.

Drop Shipping: A new method of fulfillment, in which the network marketing company handles all orders and fulfillment for its distributors from a central location, usually through an 800 number. Drop shipping frees distributors from the drudgery of stocking, tracking, and shipping inventory, allowing distributors to concentrate on selling.

Encumbered Volume: Monthly sales volume that is disqualified from being counted as part of your monthly group volume and cannot be used by you to qualify for an achievement level. Usually, volume is considered encumbered because it comes from a group or leg within your organization that has broken away or is in the process of breaking away from your personal group. For example, let's say everybody in your personal group needs to purchase a total of $3,000 worth of product per month so you can qualify for a particular achievement level. If, in a given month, one of your distributors breaks away, that distributor's volume for that month doesn't count towards your $3,000 total. The moment he breaks away, his volume is considered encumbered. If his volume is $500, that means you have to make up that $500 some other way, either by purchasing $500 of product yourself or by having one of your distributors who has not broken away buy it.

Formulation Phase: The first phase of a network marketing company's growth, acccording to Professor Charles King's four-phase system. It corresponds to the ground-floor phase.

Front End: The early, less advanced stages of a compensation plan. For example, you would say that a breakaway plan pays less on the front end, because commissions are higher after a distributor has broken away.

Frontline: Those distributors on the first level beneath you, whom you directly sponsor.

Frontloading (Front-End Loading): The practice of pressuring distributors to buy more product than they are realistically capable of selling. Usually, this is done by setting unrealistically high monthly volume requirements. There is a fine line between frontloading—which is illegal—and the legitimate setting of challenging monthly volume requirements. Ethical companies avoid frontloading by offering refunds of 70–100 percent of the cost of unsold product, and sometimes by requiring that distributors sell off a set percentage of their inventory before they are allowed to buy more.

Generation: All the distributors in a particular leg or organization; it is headed by a distributor who has broken away or achieved some other set qualification.

Generational Volume: The monthly sales volume coming from a particular generation or generational leg.

Generational Bonus: A percentage of the generational volume of a breakaway that is paid in some stairstep/ breakaway plans to that breakaway's sponsor. This is an advantageous feature because if you're paid a generational bonus on a breakaway on your sixth level, you're potentially getting paid on purchases made up to 10 or 12 levels deep.

Ground Floor: The start-up phase of a network marketing company. Ground-floor opportunities are considered attractive because they give distributors a chance to position themselves high up in the company's chain of sponsorship before the company reaches the momentum phase. However, the vast majority of ground-floor opportunities never reach momentum and do not survive. The ground-floor phase is called the Formulation phase in Professor Charles King's four-phase system.

GSV (Group Sales Volume): The total monthly volume of product sold by your entire personal group—those distributors in your organization who haven't yet broken away.

GV (Group Volume): The total monthly volume of product purchased at wholesale by your entire personal group—those distributors in your organization who haven't yet broken away.

Infinite Depth: A feature that some distributors promise their recruits. Infinite depth implies that distributors can receive commissions from an infinite number of levels. In practice, it's an illusion because comp plans offering infinite depth usually yield less money the deeper you go.

Leg: The organization of one distributor in your organization, especially one in your frontline.

Level: The measure of how far down a distributor is in an organization in relation to another distributor. For instance, if Distributor A recruits Distributor B, that means Distributor B is in Distributor A's first level. If Distributor B then recruits Distributor C, that means Distributor C is in Distributor B's first level but in Distributor A's second level. Levels are critical in understanding compensation plans because all plans specify a certain number of levels on which they "pay out." A six-level plan, for example, pays a commission only on those distributors who are six levels or less below you.

Matrix: A type of compensation plan that sets a limit on the number of people you can recruit into your frontline. (See Appendix.)

MLM/Multilevel Marketing: An older term for "network marketing." Many network marketers consider the terms "MLM" and "Multilevel Marketing" to be obsolete.

Momentum: The most rapid growth phase of a network marketing company. In momentum, sales and recruitment takes off exponentially.

Monthly Volume Requirements: Another term for "qualifications."

Network Marketing: Any form of selling that allows independent distributors to recruit other independent distributors and to draw a commission from the sales of those recruits.

Opportunity: A network marketing distributorship. When a distributor "sells the opportunity" rather than the product, that means he or she is recruiting new distributors rather than retailing product.

Opportunity Meeting: A meeting or rally held by distributors to present and sell the opportunity to potential recruits.

Organization: Distributors in your downline who fall within your pay range—that is, within those levels from which your compensation plan allows you to draw commissions.

OV (Organizational Volume): The monthly volume of product purchased by your entire organization—including your breakaway legs.

Overrides: The small percentage a distributor receives from the monthly group volume of his or her breakaway legs. Also known as "royalty."

Payout: The total percentage of revenue a network marketing company "pays out" to its distributors in commissions, overrides, and bonuses. Theoretically, the payout corresponds to the percentage of profit each distributor receives from his or her network marketing business. Percentage of payout is often used as a selling point for recruits, as in, "Company X has an 85 percent payout!" In practice, it would be hard for any company to pay out more than 60 percent without cutting its profit margins dangerously thin. Most companies that offer higher percentages usually have hidden catches or qualifiers that make it extremely difficult for any distributor to achieve the full payout. This is frustrating for distributors but necessary for company survival.

Pay Range: Those levels of your downline from which you are allowed to draw overrides and commissions.

Personal Group: Distributors in your organization who have not yet broken away.

Prospect: A person you are trying to recruit into your downline.

PV (Personal Sales Volume): The monthly volume of product that you personally sell.

PV (Personal Volume): The monthly volume of product that you personally purchase at wholesale from the company.

PV (Point Volume): Another term for bonus volume.

Qualifications: Achievement quotas that distributors must obtain to qualify for higher stairsteps, or commission levels. Qualifications can take the form of monthly group or personal volume quotas or even recruiting quotas, such as recruiting a certain number of people onto your frontline.

Qualified Executive: Another name for a distributor who has broken away.

Qualifiers: Stipulations or conditions that make it harder for distributors to achieve their monthly volume requirements. An example of a qualifier would be a stipulation tying the amount of commissions you're allowed to draw from your lower-down levels to the number of qualified executives in your frontline.

Recruiting: The act of persuading people to join your downline.

Renewal Fee: A small yearly membership fee that some companies require from their distributors. Network marketing companies are forbidden by law from making a profit from "selling" distributorships. But small annual fees are acceptable for the purpose of clearing out inactive distributors.

Retail Profit: Money earned from selling product directly to customers.

Roll-Up: A feature of some compensation plans that allows distributors to be promoted or to "roll up" above their sponsors in the organizational hierarchy. Generally, you roll up when your monthly volume exceeds that of your sponsor for a set period of time, say, two months. After you roll up above your sponsor, your sponsor no longer draws commissions from the sales of your organization. Roll-up tends to put all the top achievers together in the organization, where they can be of most benefit to one another. For example, if you're in a six-level plan and you have a high achiever down in your seventh level, the only way you'll ever draw commissions from that high achiever is if he rolls up closer to you in the hierarchy.

Royalty: Another term for overrides.

Saturation: An imaginary point at which a network marketing company exhausts the market for potential recruits, and growth stops. As with other industries, network marketing companies' growth slows down as they mature. However, true saturation is virtually impossible to achieve, and is usually just a pejorative term used by competitors to discourage potential recruits from joining a competing company, as in, "Don't join Company X. It's already saturated!"

Sponsor: A person who recruits another person into a network marketing company, then acts as the mentor to that recruit, training him or her to sell, recruit, sponsor, and train others to do the same. Can also be used as a verb, as in "to sponsor" someone.

Stability Phase: The fourth phase of a network marketing company's growth, according to Professor Charles King's four-phase system. Most companies never reach this phase. A company that survives to the stability phase is in for the long haul.

Stairstep: See Achievement Level.

Stairstep/Breakaway: A type of compensation plan in which distributors ascend "stairsteps" or achievement levels. Allows distributors to "break away" from their sponsor's group after reaching a certain achievement level. (See Appendix.)

Stockpiling: The practice of purchasing and storing more product inventory than a distributor is realistically capable of selling. Stockpiling is the natural result of frontloading.

Teleconference: A high-tech recruiting tool using telecommunications. Prospects call a certain phone number at a certain time and listen to an opportunity meeting promoting a network marketing company.

Three-Way Call: A recruiting and training strategy whereby a new, inexperienced distributor invites a prospect to participate in a phone call with the distributor and his or her sponsor. The inexperienced recruiter listens quietly and learns while the sponsor gives the sales pitch to the prospect.

Upline: People who are placed higher than a particular distributor in the sponsorship chain. Sometimes used as a synonym for *sponsor.*

Unencumbered Volume: Monthly sales volume that you are allowed to count as part of your group volume, usually because it comes from a distributor or distributors who have not yet broken away from your personal group. See Encumbered Volume.

Unilevel: A type of compensation plan in which a distributor may recruit as many people as she likes into her frontline but in which there are no breakaways.

Wave One: The first wave in the evolution of network marketing, which lasted until 1979, when the FTC ruled that Amway was a legitimate business, not a pyramid scam. Wave One was the underground or "gray-market" phase of network marketing, when the industry was in constant danger of being outlawed by overzealous regulators.

Wave Two: The second wave in the evolution of network marketing, which lasted roughly through the decade of the 1980s. This was a transitional phase, in which new technology, such as teleconferencing, voice mail, and "drop shipping" sparked an explosion in the number of network marketing companies. Most Wave-Two companies and distributors, however, failed to understand the full range of use for the new technology. Wave-Two MLM companies were often just as difficult for ordinary people to work as Wave-One companies had been.

Wave Three: The third wave in the evolution of the network marketing revolution, now in progress. It is marked by sophisticated use of management systems and technologies first developed during Wave Two. Only now are the new technologies being used at the grassroots level to make it easier for ordinary people to work the business. Wave-Three systems and technologies free distributors from the drudgery of paperwork and allow them to do what people do best—interact with other people.

Wholesale Buyer: A person who signs up as a distributor for the sole purpose of personally consuming product at the wholesale price and who does not sell the product to others. Wholesale buyers are a boon to any downline because they form a committed and dependable customer base.

Wholesale Profits: Money earned from selling product to distributors in your downline.

Width: The number of people a distributor is allowed to recruit into his or her frontline. Stairstep/breakaway and unilevel plans generally allow infinite width. Matrix plans limit width, usually to two or three people.

Index

❖

The Wave Three Way to Building Your Downline

by Richard Poe

With well over 100,000 copies in print, *Wave 3 The New Era in Network Marketing* is proof that the Wave 3 revolution has arrived to stay. Wave 3 is redefining network marketing strategy nationwide, and people want to be a part of this profitable new approach to business. With *The Wave 3 Way to Building Your Downline*, Richard Poe shows savvy network marketers how to build their own empire by using proven strategies that enable them to build a wide, deep downline—*and build it quickly*.

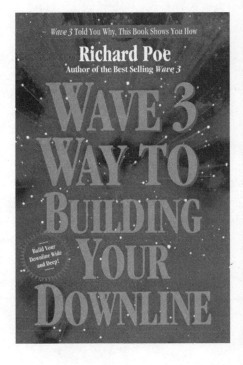

The Einstein Factor

by Win Wenger, Ph.D.
with Richard Poe

Experiments conducted in 1989 at Minnesota's Southwest State University prove that IQ can be increased 20 full points within the first 25 hours of practicing Dr. Wenger's *image streaming* technique. But *image streaming* is only one of the many simple methods Dr. Wenger has developed for creating the Einstein Factor—that dormant mental power buried deep within everyone's subconscious.

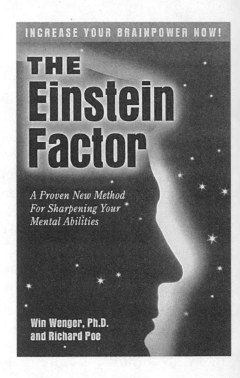

Seven Strategies for Wealth and Happiness

by Jim Rohn

Based on the bestselling Nightingale/Conant audio-cassette, this primer on the fundamental principles of success is like no other. Rohn aims to get you to understand what it means to stick to the fundamentals required for wealth and happiness. How to set goals and make goals work, the miracle of personal development, and achieving finan- 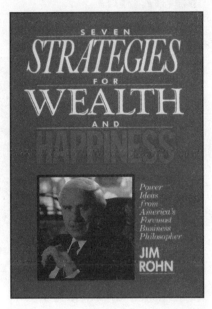 cial freedom are all addressed as the author describes the path to a richer, happier lifestyle.

How to Start Your Own Business On A Shoestring And Make Up To $500,000 A Year

by Tyler G. Hicks

Getting to $500,000 a year with little or no overhead is a dream of many entrepreneurs. Ty Hicks offers over 1,000 business ideas to spark the interest and action of his readers. He convincingly argues that the best place to work is at home and that opportunities for building riches come to those who are self-employed. To that end, Hicks explains his philosophy and encourages the reader to build wealth through his tried and tested strategies.

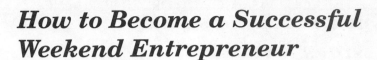

How to Become a Successful Weekend Entrepreneur

by Jennifer Basye

It is possible to add an extra $100 or more per week—without assuming the stress of a second job and working for someone else—by working as a weekend entrepreneur. Saturdays and Sundays can become income-producing days. This book offers advice from current weekend entrepreneurs as well as solid ideas that can make the difference between falling behind on the bills and saving up for a special vacation.

PRIMA PUBLISHING
P.O. Box 1260BK   Rocklin, CA 95677

USE YOUR VISA/MC AND ORDER BY PHONE
(916) 632-4400
Monday–Friday 9 A.M.–4 P.M. PST

I'd like to order copies of the following titles:

Quantity	Title Amount	
_____	*Wave Three* $14.95	_____
_____	*Seven Strategies for Wealth and Happiness* $9.95	_____
_____	*How to Become a Successful Weekend Entrepreneur* $10.95	_____
_____	*How to Start a Business* $12.95	_____
_____	*Wave 3 Way to Building Your Downline* $19.95	_____
_____	*The Einstein Factor* $15.95	_____
	Subtotal	_____
	Postage & Handling ($5 for first book, $0.50 for additional books)	_____
	7.25% Sales Tax (CA)	_____
	5% Sales Tax (IN and MD)	_____
	8.25% Sales Tax (TN)	_____
	TOTAL (U.S. funds only)	_____

Check enclosed for $_____ (payable to Prima Publishing)

HAWAII, CANADA, FOREIGN, AND PRIORITY REQUEST ORDERS, PLEASE CALL ORDER ENTRY FOR PRICE QUOTE (916) 632-4400

Charge my   ❑ MasterCard   ❑ Visa

Account No. _____   Exp. Date _____

Print Your Name _____

Your Signature _____

Address _____

City/State/Zip _____

Daytime Telephone (___) _____

Satisfaction Guaranteed!
Please allow three to four weeks for delivery.
✦ THANK YOU FOR YOUR ORDER! ✦